For the past year, I've been on a personal journey to remove busy-ness from my life. My friend Kerri provides us the perfect resource to turn down the clanging noise of chaos and set a life paced in rhythms of grace. With warmth, wisdom, and delightful teaching, this book is a treasure.

Lysa TerKeurst, *New York Times* bestselling author of *Unglued* and president of Proverbs 31 Ministries

I love and have great respect for Kerri Weems! Each visit with her leaves me sharpened and blessed. If you've ever felt overwhelmed, overworked, or overcome, Kerri Weems' important book *Rhythms of Grace* is just for you. With heartfelt maturity, Kerri beautifully reveals God's unlimited grace for every area of your life.

Amy Groeschel, co-author of S.O.A.R. Bible study for women

I'm so glad that my friend Kerri Weems wrote *Rhythms of Grace*. I believe it will help many women find their pace and hit their stride.

Lisa Bevere, Messenger International, bestselling author/minister, *Kissed the Girls and Made Them Cry*; *Fight Like a Girl*; *Lioness Arising*

In a culture that tries to get us to live at a destructive pace, my friend Kerri Weems gives us some tools to navigate the big life we lead. In *Rhythms of Grace*, Kerri tells her own story of burnout and offers all of us help in finding a healthy rhythm of life. This isn't a book that tells us to stop doing so much, or to slow down; rather, it is a book that gives practical help on how to live the expansive life that God has called us to.

Holly Wagner, pastor Oasis Church, founder GodChicks

If the pace of your life leaves you out of breath rather than energized, this book is for you. With practical insights, colorful stories, and a biblical foundation, Kerri motivates us to dive headlong into the craziness of life ... at the pace God sets.

> **Tricia Lovejoy,** SharpenHer.com, contributing writer,
> Flourish.me; wife of Shawn Lovejoy, pastor of MountainLake.tv

This is a must read! We all long for a "grace-paced" life, and in this book Kerri provides incredible wisdom and practical principles on how to discover and implement God's tempo for our lives.

> **Amy Bezet,** lead pastor's wife, Bayside Community Church

This book is an amazing resource to "recalibrate" your life. I love how Kerri gives us tools for learning God's authentic rhythm personally created for each of us. Grace makes sense on a new level!

> **Caroline Barnett,** co-pastor of Angelus Temple
> and The Dream Center

Every life has a rhythm to it. There are ups and downs, highs and lows, ins and outs. But too often, we try to set our own rhythm, forcing ourselves to live at a pace we were not created to keep. Too often we try to do all and be all. What we need to do is to slow down and keep pace with the timing God has set for us.

In *Rhythms of Grace*, my dear friend Kerri Weems reminds us in an uncompromising manner what it means to keep pace with God. Through personal reflection, humor, and authenticity, she opens her life to readers and draws us into her experiences. And with a gift that is undeniable, Kerri's insight and example remind us of what it means to live at the pace of grace in every situation in life!

> **Lisa Young,** wife of Pastor Ed Young, Fellowship Church,
> co-author, *The Creative Marriage* and *Sexperiment*; founder,
> Flavour Women's Ministry: Women Becoming World Changers

"Tired." "Worn out." "Burned out on religion." These are all outcomes we face if we don't allow Jesus to set the pace for our lives. Kerri Weems is a gifted wordsmith who tells it like it is, then brilliantly lifts our sights to a higher, unforced way of living. *Rhythms of Grace* is both powerful and practical, and a most recommended read for anyone wanting to live a significant life for Jesus.

> **Dianne Wilson,** founding pastor of Newport Church
> California; bestselling author and director of The Imagine
> Foundation

As a mom of three and a pastor's wife, I know what it's like to feel overwhelmed and off-balance. The message of Kerri's book, *Rhythms of Grace*, brings our fast-paced, perfection-driven culture back to a Christ-centered pace of life. She gives great practical tools to help us learn to enjoy every day and every season of life.

> **Holly Furtick,** wife of Pastor Steven Furtick, Elevation Church

This book, *Rhythms of Grace*, is a life-giving, practical guide to finding and living in the grace tempo designed for each one of us individually. I know this is a book I need for my life and I believe will benefit the body of Christ. Kerri lives what she teaches in this book and wants everyone to benefit from all God has taught her, so we can find our rhythm of grace too! I love it!

> **Delynn Rizzo,** Association of Related Churches

In our thirty plus years of friendship, I have always admired Kerri's consistent pursuit of growth, both personally and in her relationship with God. *Rhythms of Grace* shares beautifully simple, yet powerful principles on how to disconnect from the negative rhythms that may be influencing our pace in life and fall into step with God's divine rhythm for our lives.

> **Leslie Siebeling,** The Life Church of Memphis

For all of us who have attempted to "balance it all" and lost both ourselves and what God created us to be in the process, *Rhythms of Grace* is a must-read. Kerri brilliantly intersects our lives with wisdom and practicality for both our spiritual journeys and our run-yourself-ragged daily lives. There are few books more important to our spiritual, mental, and physical health as believers.

Lori Wilhite, author of *Leading and Loving It*; senior pastor's wife at Central Christian Church in Las Vegas

My gracious and beautiful friend Kerri Weems has an encouraging message in *Rhythms of Grace* for anyone who struggles with defining who they are through performance or accomplishments. Kerri's communication style is unique, clear, well-organized, and easy to follow. With humility and honesty, she invites us into her inner world to demonstrate how the Lord has transformed her relationship with Him to be one of a continual, refreshing fellowship of rest. When we give the Lord freedom to create order and meaning on the inside, we have confidence to make choices that are in alignment with who He designed us to be along. And the precious thing about Kerri is that this book describes exactly who she is — a woman of grace, willing by example to demonstrate how to walk in tempo with our gracious and loving Father God.

Michelle Bezet, New Life Church of Arkansas

he question I get asked more frequently than any other is "How do you balance everything?" My response is always that God's grace gets me through every season. Kerri Weems' book *Rhythms of Grace* explains this so beautifully. She gives practical examples from her own life on how you can attain peace and wholeness and how you can find your own pace of grace. I thoroughly enjoyed this book and know you will too!

Becca Ketterling, Women's Director, River Valley Church, Minneapolis

RHYTHMS OF GRACE

DISCOVERVING
GOD'S TEMPO *for*
YOUR LIFE

KERRI WEEMS

ZONDERVAN

Rhythms of Grace
Copyright © 2014 by Kerri V. Weems

This title is also available as a Zondervan ebook. Visit www.zondervan.com/ebooks.

Requests for information should be addressed to:

Zondervan, 3900 *Sparks Dr. SE, Grand Rapids, Michigan 49546*

Library of Congress Cataloging-in-Publication Data

Weems, Kerri.
  Rhythms of grace : discovering God's tempo for your life / Kerri Weems. —
1st [edition].
   pages cm
  Includes bibliographical references.
  ISBN 978-0-310-33074-5 (softcover)
   1. Time management — Religious aspects — Christianity. 2. Spiritual life —
Christianity. 3. Christian life. I. Title.
BV4598.5.W43   2014
248.4 — dc23   2014017691

Published in association with the literary agency of Fedd & Company, Inc., P.O. 341973, Austin, Texas 78734

Cover design: James Hall
Cover photography: Inspirestock / Glow Images
Interior photography: © Randy Plett Photographs / iStockphoto®
Interior illustration: © Liliboas / iStockphoto®
Interior design: Beth Shagene

First Printing July 2014 / Printed in the United States of America

This book is dedicated to Stovall.
Thank you for walking out this life
with rhythms of grace alongside me.
You are my best friend
and partner in the journey.

Contents

Foreword

The way we spend our most precious nonrenewable resource—time—causes so many of us to feel scattered, fragmented, and exhausted. Most of us are always doing more than one thing at a time and feel as if we are not doing any one thing particularly well. We seem to be always behind, always late, with one more thing, and one more thing, and one more thing to do before rushing out the door. Entire hours evaporate while we check items off our to-do lists, but when all is said and done, we still question whether the things we accomplished were truly the most important. Do the priorities on our lists and schedules match the priorities of our hearts?

No matter in what stage or season of life you find yourself, living life fruitfully requires both awareness and intentionality. If you are a mother with children still at home, there is no such thing as a normal day. If you work outside the home, you are often trying to survive without everything falling apart. If you are married, you often feel exhausted with little energy left over to invest in deepening your relationship. If you are single, setting boundaries and managing your time effectively present their own unique challenges. Yet, so often we feel like we are running as fast as we can and getting nowhere. Eventually, we cannot keep up with the relentless pace of our own lives, so we end up burned out or quitting.

If we are ever to tap into the abundant life that Jesus came to give us, we must stop the overwhelming momentum of the lives we have created for ourselves. We have to learn to listen and move to a different beat. This is why you need to read this book. Jesus wants us not only to run our race, but also to finish it. If we learn to tap into what my friend Kerri calls the "rhythms of grace," we will find all that we need to do and be all that we are called be.

I read this book in one sitting and found myself constantly nodding in agreement. In this day of twenty-four-hour connection and incessant demands on our time, I cannot think of a better book to read. You will discover what it means to experience rhythms of grace and how to find God's tempo for your life. There is a pace for your race, and that is where you will discover his grace.

Christine Caine
Founder, The A21 Campaign
Bestselling author, *Undaunted*

Acknowledgments

To Stovall, Kaylan, Stovie, and Annabelle: I couldn't have written this book without your love and support. There were lots of "mom-less" nights when I stayed up late to write in the study and mornings I slept in while you guys went to school. Thank you for your grace and patience in the process.

To my mom, Karen, my dad, Joe, and my sister, Darla: You all read through the manuscript and heard me talk about it ad nauseam until you probably couldn't stand it anymore. Thank you for believing in me and praying for me through the process.

To the Celebration Church staff and Celebration Sisterhood: Thank you for being generous in releasing me to write and walk out the message of this book. You have graciously allowed me to lead you and grow into the woman I am today.

To the friends who came alongside and helped me in the editorial process: Chari Orozco, Linda Riddle, Lexie Goodman, Jenny Huang, Molly Venzke, Jeff Jenkins, and Joel Miller. Your insightful feedback and assistance with edits truly helped to shape this book.

To Sandy, my editor: Thank you for believing in the book

project. You cared enough to make thorough edits of the manuscript and helped this book become its best.

To Esther, my agent: Thank you for believing in me and the message of this book.

To Julia Mateer and Paul Wilbur: Your professional feedback regarding aspects of emotional health and Jewish history and customs was invaluable.

Chapter 1

The Pace of Grace

Get away with me and you'll recover your life. . . . Walk with me and work with me — watch how I do it. Learn the unforced rhythms of grace. . . . Keep company with me and you'll learn to live freely and lightly.

Matthew 11:28–30 MSG

The bell rang on the first day of school and the students began filing in. Excited chatter mixed, with sighs of resignation, floated from the hallways into the makeshift classroom of a temporary building. *I had no idea the administration had given me such a big class for first period,* I thought. *I need to make sure I have enough material to keep all these kids busy or the next fifty minutes are going to be a disaster!* When I looked down at my desk, I came to the devastating realization that I had left my lesson planner and all of my materials at home. I panicked and my mind went blank. I couldn't remember what I was supposed to teach. How would I make it through the day with no lesson plans?

If you have ever been a high school teacher, you will understand what I'm about to say. High school students are wild creatures.

They detect unpreparedness the way a shark smells blood. They can sniff it out a mile away, and when they do, they go in for the kill. They will gather in packs. They will mark you as prey, and they will circle you, looking for a moment of weakness. When they find it, they will strike quickly, mercilessly, and relentlessly. You will bleed out hall passes and discipline slips until you are dry, and at the end of the day the janitor will sweep your depleted body off the floor with the pencil dust and little paper circles from the three-hole punch. As a teacher, my greatest ally is my lesson plan book. I had left mine at home, and now I was cast adrift in a hostile sea. I imagined the rest of my day, bluffing my way through each lecture. The next seven hours would be miserable.

The small, stuffy room was filled to capacity. Some kids were even sitting on the floor. *This has to be a violation of some kind of code,* I thought angrily. *There's no way I can manage a class this size.* I had stepped out from behind the desk, steeling my will to take on the challenge ahead, when the room fell suddenly and completely silent. *What is going on?* Through the open window I could hear the sound of the lawn mower grooming the football field and releasing that distinctive smell of summer, the scent of cut grass. A breeze began to blow through the room, providing welcome relief from the muggy morning heat. The tension of the moment hung in the air for what seemed like an hour. The mower, the green smell of fresh grass, and the gentle breezes held my senses hostage until I realized I was feeling the breezes somewhere I should not be feeling them — my upper thighs. The students' escalating snickers jerked me back into reality just as I looked down in horror to find I had forgotten more than my lesson plans that day. I had forgotten my pants!

And then I woke up.

It had all been a dream ... a particular kind of recurring nightmare I'd had for several weeks. These dreams all revolved around similar themes: being overwhelmed, being out of control, or missing an important deadline like college exams or, as I had just experienced, being unprepared for the first day of school. *Why wouldn't they just go away?*

I looked around the room to get my bearings. My husband was sleeping peacefully next to me, his chest rhythmically rising and falling with each breath. The moonlight peeking through the shades revealed I was safe—there were no students in the room waiting to mock me into oblivion for forgetting my pants. All was well. I sat up and looked at the clock near my bed and discovered it was 2:45 a.m. The sun was not up yet, thank goodness! I lay back down on my pillow, relieved I could indulge in almost four more hours of blissful sleep.

Unfortunately, sleep escaped my grasp that night—and it wasn't the first time. Until recently, I had always been the "sleepy one" in the family. By 9:00 p.m., I was usually the one stomping grumpily around the house, turning off the lights and the TV. I was the one gathering up the cell phones for the night and shooing everyone into their rooms so I could fall into bed. Now, all of a sudden, everyone was begging *me* to turn out the lights. I was unable to settle down in the evenings regardless of how tired I felt. I hid under the covers and played word games on my iPhone long after the lights went out. I woke suddenly for no apparent reason throughout the night. And, like this particular night, I wanted to go to back to sleep—I tried to—but the adrenaline rush that woke me up kept my mind and body in a state of high alert until the sun came up and the alarm went off.

As I lay there trying to fall back to sleep, I thought about this persistent and unwelcome disruption to my routine. I hadn't felt like myself in months. Why was I so out of whack? It was mid-November and the year was coming to a close, but in some ways I felt as if it had never really taken place. The months had flown by with one major transition after another. We had moved into a new house and immediately discovered a mold (and rodent!) infestation that took over a year to repair. My husband and I were both busier than we'd ever been, and we were finding it increasingly difficult to keep up with breakneck schedules and overlapping deadlines. All of these things—the good and the bad—began to take on a life of their own. I constantly felt I was forgetting something important . . . and usually I was. I just couldn't manage all the competing demands anymore. I felt like a hamster running on a wheel I couldn't keep pace with, and I didn't know how to jump off.

For the first time since planting our church, I felt like I wanted to quit. It's not that I didn't love our church . . . I did. It's not that I wasn't grateful . . . I was. But at that moment, my ministry commitments seemed like the only negotiable things left on the table. I already felt as if I was throwing cargo over the side of a rapidly sinking ship, and even the valuable boxes were fair game. I never thought I would feel that way. I never really understood it when other people felt that way, although I always tried to be encouraging and helpful. And yet, here I was, ready to throw in the towel on everything I had spent the last fifteen years of my life helping to build. I was ready to walk away and never look back.

It was such a lonely place to be, too. Nobody, not even my husband, knew how I was feeling. I believed that telling anyone I was ready to quit would seem selfish and weak. On top of the stress was the guilt of knowing that what people saw on the outside was not the person I was on the inside. I was living a double life, but I was tired of the charade. I didn't want to fake it anymore; I just wanted to let it go. The funny thing is, letting it all go was just exactly what I needed to do. In fact, *it's just exactly what I ultimately did.* Only, I didn't let go by walking away from it all. I let go by learning to lean into God's grace and finding His divine rhythm for my life. It just took me a few more weeks to get there.

The moment finally came in our first church service of the new year. My husband, Stovall, was teaching a message called "Project or Process?" As he spoke, I clearly heard God speak to me for the first time in months. *Kerri, you are not a project; you are My child. Our relationship is not a project; it is a covenant. Your life with Me is a forever commitment. I'm fully committed to you for eternity. Will you commit fully to a lifetime with Me?*

Imagine you are married to a pastor and serve on the executive team of a church of twelve thousand people, and the Lord asks you if you will commit to a lifetime of living for Him. Of course, I had already made that commitment a long time ago. I became a believer in Christ when I was eight years old, and although my walk with Him has not been perfect (whose is?), it has been consistent. No, salvation was not the issue behind the words the Holy Spirit spoke to my heart. Neither were they words of rebuke or a command to commit to greater devotional disciplines. Instead, the Spirit's words to me were simply an invitation — an invitation to view everything in my life, including my relationship with God, through the lens of a sustainable, lifelong rhythm.

It was an invitation Jesus first gave to weary souls over two millennia ago:

Are you tired? Worn out? Burned out on religion? Come to me. Get away with me and you'll recover your life. I'll show you how to take a real rest. Walk with me and work with me — watch how I do it. Learn the unforced rhythms of grace. I won't lay anything heavy or ill-fitting on you. Keep company with me and you'll learn to live freely and lightly. (Matthew 11:28 – 30 MSG)

Tired. Worn out. Burned out on religion. All of those words applied to the state I was in. And you know what? *Recover your life ... real rest ... unforced ... free and light living.* These were the kinds of words that described exactly the state of being I wanted to live in but could never quite attain. I wanted a lifestyle of unbroken fellowship with Jesus. I wanted to learn to live in the rhythms of grace. And more than anything, I wanted Jesus to set the pace for my life.

Since that first Sunday of the new year when God reminded me that our relationship was a covenant and not a project, God has been teaching me more about what it means to walk in time with Him. As we travel together through the pages of this book, I'll share how I learned, and continue to learn, what it means to allow God to set the pace for my life. In the process, my prayer is that I can be a friend to you as you discover your own rhythms of grace.

Let the Music Move You

Rhythms of grace are God's divine tempo for your life. But before we talk more about what that means, we need to consider the nature of rhythm itself as well as our most basic response to it, which is *movement*. Sometimes while I'm grocery shopping, I suddenly realize I have been tapping my fingers on the cart in response to a song that's being played in the store. When I'm waiting in my car stopped at a traffic signal and someone pulls up next to me with their windows down and the bass booming through their speakers, I start to bob my head, to my kids' extreme embarrassment! I'm not trying to embarrass them, I just can't help it — I respond to music with movement.

I have a few playlists on my iPod that I listen to when I'm working out. There are different kinds of music for different kinds of movement. When I engage in the slow and sustained movements of stretching, I like to listen to the ethereal tunes of Enya or piano instrumentals. But when it comes to cardio workouts, Enya won't do. I need energy! I need motivation! I need speed!

So I pump Lecrae into my headphones. Why? Because the rhythm makes me move. How I move—the speed, the motion, the duration—is a response to the beat I am listening to. The rhythm of the music sets my workout pace, but when it comes to the pace of my life, I have to ask, *Who is setting the rhythm?* The answer depends on who has access to my ears, my mind, and my heart in that moment.

What music is playing the loudest in your ears right now? How would you describe your "movements" in response to that music? The answers to these questions matter because they provide an essential clue about who—or what—is setting the rhythm for your life. For example, are your movements through this season of life timid and hesitant? Perhaps the voice of insecurity has access to your ears. Are your movements disjointed and chaotic? Maybe guilt or fear is playing the theme song of your life. Or perhaps, like me, your movements have taken on a crazy momentum of their own. You're not sure who is setting the pace, but you know you're out of control.

Looking back, it's clear to me that I had been on the path toward burnout for a while. Over a period of two years, I had allowed myself to listen to some pretty destructive music. I was moving in response to rhythms set by ambition, fear, guilt, insecurity, and perfectionism (to name just a few).

People have different responses when it comes to dealing with the demands of life. Some people hop on the hamster wheel and keep going faster and faster, as if they can outrun the stress or even run away from it. Some people feel so helpless and out of control that they just stop moving altogether. Maybe you are the type of person who ignores problems in the hope that they will somehow magically go away. I understand each of those reactions—and I have experienced them plenty of times! Scripture exhorts us to "run with endurance the race that is set before us" (Hebrews 12:1

NASB). We can't do that standing still, nor can we do it if we are so drained and frazzled that we collapse before we even see the finish line.

Endurance running is all about running at the right pace, and to finish strong each runner needs to find her own tempo. Somewhere between the hamster wheel and the full stop there is a perfect pace, a rhythm that is a custom fit for your life and the leg of the race you are running right now. This perfect pace is God's tempo for your life, His perfect rhythm. His grace is what gives you the freedom and power to find that rhythm and walk in it. Finding that rhythm and keeping pace with it is the key to running the race of life and faith with endurance until you cross the finish line.

What Rhythms of Grace Are — And Are *Not*

So what does it mean to experience rhythms of grace, to find God's tempo for our lives? It means we create space in our days, weeks, and months for spiritual and emotional renewal. We allow our relationship with God to structure our lives and mark out their rhythm. One way to understand how such sacred rhythms work is to consider how holiday rhythms work.

Every culture in the world operates according to an annual rhythm set, in large part, by its seasons and holidays. In the United States, Labor Day, followed by Thanksgiving, Christmas, and New Year's Day punctuate the first part of the school year with rhythm. In my family, during the school year we march to the beat of busy days for several weeks, but we always look forward to the next holiday—the promised *fermata* that provides a welcome pause in the *tempo staccato* of our daily schedules.

Many annual holidays around the world were originally set by the church calendar and, thus, were referred to as *holy days*. Over time, the two words got smashed together to give us the word *holidays*, but the modern term no longer carries the associations with sacred moments. Don't get me wrong. I love seeing my family, cooking huge meals, wrapping and giving gifts, decorating the house—even all the extra busyness these seasons bring. But as much as I love the fall and winter holidays, they do not mark out a *sacred* rhythm. If we desire a life that moves to the rhythms of grace, then sacred rhythms—rhythms set to God's tempo for us—must mark out the measure of our years and create space for our bodies, minds, and spirits to be refreshed and renewed. That's what rhythms of grace are—a spiritual structure for rest and restoration.

How, then, are we to establish sacred rhythms for our lives? And what should we do in those holy spaces in time? In the chapters that follow, we'll explore several aspects of the grace-paced life and consider some practical ways to use them. However, it's important first to acknowledge some potential misconceptions by saying what rhythms of grace are *not*.

Rhythms of grace are *not* primarily about:

- *Time management.* We will have to consider how we use our time, but that is not the focus. Instead, our focus is on how to see time for what it is—eternity in disguise. The pace of our lives *is* sacred. Our time on this earth is fleeting, yet our lives *are* eternal. What we do on the temporal side has an impact on the eternal side.

- *Discipline.* Discipline will be required, but it is not the goal.

- *Habits.* You will likely develop new habits, but they will serve as a framework for something deeper.

- *Withdrawing from the world to engage in spiritual practices.* You will engage in spiritual practices, to be sure, but they will set the tone of your everyday life instead of being something separate and compartmentalized.

- *Saying no and setting boundaries.* The discernment and strength you need in order to do these things will emerge from the rhythms of grace, but they are not the starting point.

To be clear, all of these things *are* part of a grace-paced life, but they are not the main idea. They are simply external structures that reflect the pace that God's grace has set for our lives—we must not mistake them for the goal. The way we approach these things will and should change in every season of life. Some habits change when we go from being in school to working. The way we manage our time might shift when we go from being single to being married. When we add children to the mix, we have to adjust the way we approach our spiritual disciplines if we are going to have any hope at all of having spiritual disciplines! However, no matter how the demands we face in each season of life change, our goal of staying in step with Christ remains the same.

God did not create one person exactly the same as another. He has a unique design, plan, and purpose for all of the billions of people living on earth. Different people can even sing the same song and it will sound slightly different. This is because each person interprets and expresses things in a one-of-a-kind way. Regardless of how different our life contexts may be, I believe we can all enter into rhythms of grace in a way that authentically reflects the way God created us to function in this season of our lives. It *is* possible.

What's in Store

If you flip back and look at the contents page, you will see that this book is divided into three parts. In part 1, we explore the three foundational components for sacred rhythms—*Shalom*, Sabbath, and Grace.

In part 2, we explore pacesetters and peace stealers. We'll learn some empowering truths about new ways to live—ways that honor rest and make it the baseline beat that sets the rhythm of our lives in work, relationships, physical health, and spiritual vitality.

In part 3, we dive into practical strategies for managing time, relationships, and other significant factors that affect the pace of our lives. We will also consider how we can sustain these new, positive changes.

If you're like me, you might be tempted to jump straight to "fixing it," whatever "it" may be for you. But I encourage you not to skip over the first parts of this book in order to get to the "how-to" part. Instead, I invite you to look at this as a process to be engaged in rather than a project to be completed. If you are willing to value the process as much as the outcome, I believe you will achieve much greater clarity about the things that are weighing you down, and you will also find the freedom and confidence to let them go—for good.

Remember that this is not a performance grid to impose on your life. And even though I am sharing my journey with you, keep in mind that what I share is simply what works for me. Applying these principles will likely look different in your life than it does in mine, and that's fine. Part of the beauty of rhythms of grace is their adaptability. Take your time, absorb what you read, reread parts that stand out to you, and give yourself permission to establish your own rhythms of grace.

My hope is that the message in this book is one you will refer back to again and again as the seasons of your life change. I pray that as you begin to listen and respond to the Holy Spirit, you will discover God's divine tempo for your life. My heart's desire is that you will go the full distance of your race, and not just so you can crawl exhausted across the finish line. I want you to enjoy the race and come to the end with your head held high, a smile on your face, and your arms lifted in a double fist-punch! And, my friend, getting to that moment is all about pacing yourself now for the long run.

In the next chapter, we'll consider the core principle of the rhythms of grace lifestyle, which is wholeness. The word the Bible uses for this kind of wholeness is *shalom*, and it is the starting point for creating a sustainable pace. Before we can even begin to think about clearing out our schedules and making health and relationships a priority, we have to know what kind of people Jesus has called us to be and become attuned to the leading of the Holy Spirit as we build our daily lives—which eventually add up to our whole lives.

For Reflection

Rhythms of Grace is designed to guide you through a process that will help you to identify and establish new rhythms for your life. As part of that process, each chapter includes questions to help you make connections between your life and the teaching in that chapter. You will notice that one particular question is repeated at the end of every chapter: "What do you sense the Holy Spirit might be saying to you?" The reason this question is repeated is because taking time to listen to the promptings of the Holy Spirit is how we get the right "music" in our ears—it's how we learn to move in response to His timing and His perfect pace. If we fail to listen for the sound of His voice and then to respond to the words He speaks, we cannot hope to move to the rhythms of grace. Taking time to briefly write down your responses to these questions will be a great help to you when we get to chapter 10, "Reboot Your Schedule." There, you'll have a chance to reflect back on what you wrote, which will help you begin to do the practical work of constructing your annual, weekly, and daily rhythms.

Get ready to step into the rhythms of grace!

1. How do you feel after reading this chapter?

2. What parts of this chapter relate to your life?

3. What do you hope to take away from reading *Rhythms of Grace*?

4. What do you sense the Holy Spirit might be saying to you?

THE FOUNDATIONS
OF RHYTHM

IN ORDER TO BUILD A LIFE CHARACTERIZED BY SACRED RHYTHMS, we need to understand three foundational principles — *Shalom*, Sabbath, and Grace. *Shalom* is an inner experience of well-being that overflows into our outer world. When we are living in *shalom*, we worry less about managing time and setting boundaries and focus instead on living authentically from the inside out.

Sabbath is the baseline beat in God's rhythm of rest. There is a hidden message in the biblical command to observe the Sabbath that might surprise you and change the way you think about rest altogether. I know that was the case for me!

Grace, as we will explore it here, is the experience of being yoked to Christ. God calls each of us to a purpose that is expressed, in large part, by our daily work. Yet, isn't that same work usually the biggest contributor to the frantic and chaotic pace of our lives? The gift of grace is that when we are yoked to Christ and fall in step with His rhythm, our daily work is no longer at odds with wholeness and rest.

Chapter 2

Shalom: Everything As It Should Be

I'm leaving you well and whole.
That's my parting gift to you. Peace.

John 14:27 MSG

When I was a young girl, my grandmother went through various hobby phases. One time she got into CB radios. It must have been the influence of that old Burt Reynolds movie *Smokey and the Bandit*. She saw that movie one weekend, and a few nights later she had a huge CB radio sitting on the kitchen counter and had struck up random conversations with truckers all over the Southeast. She was never shy about trying new hobbies, and she usually managed to rope my grandfather into trying them too.

One of her more traditional hobbies was putting together jigsaw puzzles, and I don't mean the little two-hundred-piece kind. I'm talking about the kind of puzzles with a thousand or more pieces. One day I walked into her kitchen and the CB radio was gone. Instead, there were thousands of tiny puzzle pieces lying on top of the breakfast table. I had seen puzzles before, but never one with so many pieces. Each little fragment held a tiny brushstroke of color, and each one was cut in a unique shape. Not one piece could be fit together randomly or unintentionally. Just looking at all those little disorganized bits of puzzle board lying there in a pile of chaos made me start to stress out. (And I was only eleven!)

"Grandma, how in the world are you going to finish this puzzle?" I asked. "The pieces are so tiny, and there are so many of them."

From the corner behind the table she pulled out the box the puzzle came in and pointed to the top of it. "Well, Kerri, the picture on the top of this box is what I'm trying to make. I just keep fitting the pieces together until they match the picture," she said.

"But won't that take a long time?" I protested.

"Yes, it probably will," she said. "I guess I will just have to be patient with the process and learn as I go."

The picture on the top of the box helped her sort through the pieces of the puzzle by reminding her of what she was trying to create. It showed her the big picture—the end goal—so she could make sense of all the little pieces she was working with at any given moment. My grandma wasn't overwhelmed with the puzzle because, amid all of the little pieces scattered everywhere, she could see the big picture.

We all have multiple pieces that make up our lives, and at times those pieces seem like they just don't fit together. How do our jobs or daily tasks connect to our family relationships? How do our family relationships fit together with our church commitments? What about the marriage piece—where does that go? And the finance piece? And the friendship piece? Where do all of these different pieces of life fit, and what's the big picture we're supposed to be looking at while piecing them together?

Wouldn't it be nice if we had something like a puzzle box top with a picture of the "good life" on it—a life of meaning, purpose, peace, and fulfillment—that we could look to as a guide as we assemble the various pieces of our lives? Wouldn't it be reassuring to know that the picture we are assembling day by day, year by year, is going to add up to something beautiful when it is all said and done?

The good news is that we *do* have something like this to guide us. The even better news is that the image on the box top is the masterpiece of God's original intent for us, which is *shalom*. *Shalom* is the big picture we must look to if we want to put the pieces of our lives together with meaning and order. It's the first thing we need to explore when we consider moving into a grace-paced life.

Meaning and Order

What word comes to mind when you hear the phrase *rhythms of grace*? For some, it might be the word *peace*. This is especially true for those of us who are feeling overwhelmed and unfocused. In those moments, all I want is a little peace!

But what is peace really, and what does it look like? Does it mean that I have no conflict in my life? I would have to move out into the mountains and live like a hermit away from the rest of the world for that to happen. Just the fact that I am married and have three kids (and a dog!) makes this impossible.

Peace is much more than the absence of trouble. It's even more than experiencing a feeling of surpassing calm during times of stress and trial. Peace, the way it is described in the Bible, is one aspect of a much bigger and more complete picture of wholeness.

Shalom is the Hebrew word for "peace." Most of us have heard the word *shalom* and understand its general meaning. What used to come to my mind was simply the absence of conflict, hardship, or stress—a perfect state of calm and serenity. When I read the

Scriptures or heard sermons about Jesus being the Prince of Peace, I translated that to mean that as long as I was obedient to Him, my life would have minimal levels of stress and conflict. Conversely, I interpreted feeling stressed or experiencing conflict as a lack of peace. What's interesting about this notion of peace is how unbiblical it is. Think about it. Jesus' life was not at all free from hardship, stress, or conflict. Based on my misguided definition, even Christ did not walk in perfect peace! So what is the meaning of the *shalom* kind of peace found all throughout the Scriptures? The answer starts in Genesis.

The well-known words "in the beginning" open Act 1 of the Bible with the most sweeping, epic drama ever played out—the saga of God and humankind. Before one star lit the sky, before one blade of grass sprung up from the new earth, the Bible tells us that the earth was "formless and empty." The Hebrew word for "formless" is *tohu*. The short definition? Waste. There was no order, no life, no night or day. Just the chaotic wasteland of "the deep" and the Spirit of God hovering over it (Genesis 1:2). How long the earth was in this suspended state is anyone's guess, but what changed it all was a sound—the sound of God's own voice penetrating the void.

When God spoke into the formless chaos, something amazing happened. Meaning and order began to emerge in the midst of the void. Like the maestro calling the orchestra to attention, God commands, "Let there be light!" Then He begins to conduct a symphony so grand, complex, and intricate that it echoes throughout all the ages of humankind on the earth. In the opening passages of the Bible, you can almost feel the emerging rhythm of creation. Each day begins with a new creation (land, sea, plants, animals), which is then crowned with approval ("God saw that it was good"), and is followed by night and rest. And so the pattern continues until the sixth day.

The symphony of heaven culminates in the pinnacle of creation: human beings. Adam and Eve are placed in the middle of the garden of Eden with order and beauty all around. They receive authority to act as God's regents, His royally appointed stewards, over everything. Fruitfulness and increase are the rule. There is no death, only life. No disease, only health. No family drama, no power struggles, no abuse. Prosperity and justice are not at odds with each other. Such an idea was inconceivable because, in God's world, prosperity and justice are one and the same.

The world we see in Eden is a world characterized by *shalom*. *Shalom* is Eden's "normal," its fabric, and its outcome. *Shalom* is God's box-top picture of the good life. It is a state of abundant well-being and complete wholeness from top to bottom — nothing missing, nothing lost. *Shalom*, in other words, is the way things are supposed to be.[1]

When it comes to ordering our own lives, *shalom* is the picture we are looking at and aiming for, but it's nowhere remotely close to the world we live in. With the fall of Adam and Eve, the image of God in human beings was shattered into a billion pieces, each fragment containing a tiny bit of the original masterpiece. We have the pieces, but not the box top — it was lost when the image was shattered. So how can the pieces be put back together?

The good news is that through His death and resurrection, Jesus gave us the hope and authority to reclaim a state of wholeness and fullness for our lives, a state of *shalom*. Just as my grandma looked to the top of the box as a model for reconstructing the image on her puzzle, we can look to the model of Jesus to put the pieces of our lives together. He is our box-top big picture — the perfect image of the life God intended for us from the beginning — thanks to Jesus, we can still have that life in great measure.

When God wanted to bring order out of chaos and create the universe, He spoke, "Let there be light!" When He wanted to bring a once-and-for-all solution to the problem of fallen humanity, He spoke grace and truth in Jesus Christ. The prophet Isaiah said of Christ, "But He was wounded for our transgressions, He was bruised for our iniquities; the chastisement for our peace [shalom] was upon Him, and by His stripes we are healed" (Isaiah 53:5 NKJV). If God had stopped at redeeming us, if He had only covered our sin and opened the door of heaven just wide enough for us to squeeze in by the skin of our teeth, it would have been enough. But God is so gracious that He went way beyond the bare minimum. He wants us to be agents of His message on this earth, not only through the words we speak, but also through the lives we live. So in addition to His marvelous redemption, He returned to us what was lost in Eden—the gift of *shalom*.

But life doesn't feel like that often, does it?

When life feels chaotic, our attempts to reclaim order and wholeness usually start with something external. I used to have a little ritual I turned to when my world felt like it was spinning out of control. I packed my laptop into the car and drove to Office Max, where I bought a brand new, undefiled calendar. Then I drove to the nearest Starbucks and drank my body weight in caffeine while I made lists of every single thing in my life—every project, every deadline, every relationship, important dates, upcoming projects, possible projects, my exercise plan, my diet plan. I turned my whole life into lists and plotted it onto an organizational grid.

For a few weeks, my little life grid made me feel better. It was nice to see all the puzzle pieces neatly arranged into categories. It looked beautiful on paper. Simple. Elegant. Clean. Like living in some kind of Apple® Store universe. But real life is nothing like that, and *real life* is where I *really live*. It's anything but simple, elegant, and clean, and nothing like an Apple Store. It's usually more like Wal-Mart—complicated, awkward, and messy. (No disrespect, Wal-Mart. I love your butter rotisserie chicken. It has saved family dinner on many a night.) Real life is oblivious to my master plan and project timelines.

My kids, for example, actually have the nerve to get sick on the very day I have a curriculum deadline. *Kids, really? You couldn't wait one more day to get a cold? Tomorrow would have been a perfect day to stay home!*

My friends' babies have the audacity to be born days before their due dates. *Hello, little baby. Don't you realize I have you penciled in for Thursday? This is most inconvenient.*

My husband has the gall to disrupt my schedule by whisking me away on a surprise overnighter to the beach. *Hon, date night is not until Friday. Didn't you look at the master calendar? So inconsiderate.*

My life plan was getting in the way of actually *living my life*.

If you are cringing a little bit on the inside about how dysfunctional all this sounds, it's okay. It *is* dysfunctional. Most people see being organized as a strength—and it is—but any overused strength turns into a weakness. I was using my organizational gifts to put my outer world in order when the real problem was with my inner world. You see, disorder on the outside is almost always a reflection of disorder on the inside. My outer world kept getting out of control because my inner world was out of order.

Jesus wasn't just blowing off steam when He told the Pharisees, "First clean the inside of the cup and dish, and then the outside also will be clean" (Matthew 23:26). Like me, the Pharisees were trying to fix an inner problem with outward performance. They were trying to make up for the brokenness and dysfunction in their hearts by overperforming acts of religious piety. I was trying to make up for my self-doubt and fear of failure by overperforming ... everything. I finally learned that I couldn't fix what's wrong on the inside by addressing only what was wrong on the outside. That's why time management systems, spiritual disciplines, and health plans aren't enough—you won't bring long-term order to your outer world until there is order in your inner world.

Three Characteristics of *Shalom*

In his book *The Seven Habits of Highly Effective People*, author Stephen Covey defines habit number 2 in this way: "Begin with the end in mind." As we take steps to connect the pieces of our lives, we begin with the end in mind by keeping our focus on the box top of *shalom*. But having an image or idea about something and realizing it are two different things. So if Jesus invites us to live in *shalom*, how do we accept the invitation? In other words, how will we know when we've found it? How can we tell when we are experiencing it? Although *shalom* might take several different forms, I want to share three characteristics that describe how I have come to recognize and experience *shalom* in the context of my everyday life. Perhaps these characteristics can be a starting point to help you begin to recognize *shalom* in your life.

1. *I experience shalom when I am fully present and fully aware in the moment.* How many people or things get your undivided —whole—attention? If you think about it, it's likely a rare occurrence that you are ever fully focused on just one thing. "Multitasking" is a performance buzzword, and I used to wear my multitasking badge as proof of how efficient and productive I could be. However, recent studies show that multitasking is not really beneficial. Splitting your attention between several activities at once causes the quality of your work to suffer. I would also add that it causes the quality of your life to suffer.

I had so conditioned myself to divide my attention between multiple things that I actually felt bored focusing on just one thing. No matter what I was doing with my body, my mind was always otherwise occupied. In church, I would start off taking sermon notes, but within a couple of minutes the margins of my note paper gave birth to shopping lists, project timelines, reminders of people to talk to after the service, notes about things that could be improved for the next service ... you name it. I still wrote down all the points and Scriptures, but I didn't relax into the moment and really take it in. My body was in the sanctuary, but I was far from being fully present and fully aware of what was happening there.

I was always thinking about the next thing to be done or the one thing that wasn't done. I tried to listen to my kids' accounts of their days at school, but I was too often distracted by thoughts of things like getting dinner started, which left me in a hazy state because I was never fully invested anywhere. My diluted attention in the moment also left me with diluted memories. Even though I know there is no condemnation in Christ and I don't beat myself up about this, I do have regrets. And I'm so glad I have learned to understand the value of undivided attention.

I know now that I am experiencing *shalom* when what is happening with the people in front of me at any given moment is the focus of my thoughts, my emotions, and my energy. I am relaxed, making eye contact, curious about what they are saying (and not just mentally formulating my own response). I ask questions when I don't understand instead of hastily drawing conclusions. And you know what I have come to realize? Ten minutes of focusing in the moment leaves me feeling emotionally, spiritually, and mentally richer and fuller than ten hours of multitasking and splitting my attention between a thousand different things.

If you have been juggling too much for too long, the practice of being fully invested in the moment might feel strange at first. It still doesn't always come naturally to me. I have to remind myself to stop trying to hurry the conversation along. Sometimes I have to stop my hands physically from absentmindedly scrolling through Instagram when I have a free moment. But the more I practice, the easier and more natural it feels for me. And it will come to feel the same way for you. As I continue to reclaim *shalom* wholeness in my life, I am getting better and better at giving this gift to others.

2. I experience shalom when there is alignment between my outer world and my inner world. How many times have you said yes to something and instantly regretted it? How many times have you found yourself looking forward to a relaxing weekend only to remember—with a sense of dread rather than excitement—that you committed to multiple engagements? Or maybe your boss asked you to do a project outside of your regular work schedule, and you said yes but you would rather be at home with your family. Maybe you signed up your kids for four or five different after-school activities when you knew that even one or two would push the limits of your schedule. *How did I end up here again?* you think. *Burned out. Exhausted. Grouchy.*

When our inner and outer worlds are out of alignment, we experience dissonance. Choices that clash with our beliefs or values create tension in our lives. In my case, the tension has often been between my public life and my private life. The private me, my core personality, is an introverted intellectual. And not just a little bit introverted; I'm ridiculously introverted! Like an absent-minded professor, I'm constantly lost in my thoughts—and I like it there! But the public me is a partner in a major ministry—a ministry that requires significant and routine interaction with people. See any problems there? Like many women, I sometimes feel like what I do does not necessarily bring out the best of who I am.

To find *shalom* I have to be intentional about finding ways and places to bring harmony to these two aspects of the life God has called me to. I had to accept who God created me to be—flaws, weaknesses, shortcomings, and all. I had to learn to rest in God's grace and stop measuring my value as a person by how I performed. I also had to respect my need for solitude and reflection and schedule them into my life. By giving myself permission to honor those needs as part of who I am, I experience *shalom*—alignment between my inner and outer worlds.

Shalom doesn't require perfection, but when we are moving in the direction of *shalom,* we make decisions that close rather than widen the gap between who we are, what we believe and value, and what we actually do.

3. *I experience shalom when I focus on wholeness, not productivity.* On one of those occasions when I was sitting in Starbucks rearranging the pieces of my life into a grid, I was trying to create peace by imposing order and structure on my life. What are structures, really? They have a vital function—as vessels designed to hold something else—but they are not what's most important. For example, scaffolding is a structure designed to support a building while it is in the process of being built. Once the building is completed, no one wants to see the scaffolding—they want to see the building! To take it a step further, even the building is a structure designed to hold something else. No matter however lovely the architecture might be on the outside, the reason for the building's existence is whatever is going on inside it. If it's an office building, then the work inside, not the building, is what is of true value. If it's a home, then the life inside it, not the brick and mortar, is what matters most.

My problem was that the structure and order I was trying to impose on my life was designed to contain things like productivity, efficiency, and achievement, but not peace. I stuffed as much productivity into my structures as they could contain, and then expanded them as much as I could to contain more. The better my life management systems were, the more productive I could be. But I was using the wrong box top as my guide—my tactics would never lead to the peace and wholeness I was looking for. Is it any wonder that, for all of my organizing and systematizing, my world still felt chaotic?

Depending on who you are, increased productivity might be easy or it might be hard. Either way, it misses the point. *Shalom* isn't about doing more. It's about experiencing more of God's peace in the midst of all the things we have to do.

Pursuing Peace

The goal of establishing and maintaining rhythms of grace is to become whole persons—not perfect persons, but whole persons. It's a process of making intentional decisions that enable us, over time, to reclaim *shalom*, which is a state of abundant well-being and wholeness. Maybe *shalom* wholeness seems so far removed from where you are right now that you can't even imagine what it would be like to feel whole. Maybe your life is fractured into a billion pieces at the moment. If so, I need you to hold on to hope and to trust that the God who brought order and meaning to the universe in creation is the same God who can bring order and meaning to the wastelands of your life.

Jesus is *sar shalom*, the Prince of Peace (Isaiah 9:6). Peace is His domain, and it is His to bestow. God *wants* us to live in *shalom*—wholeness—and He made provision for it in Christ. The depth and breadth of God's provision show us that salvation is not only for heaven, but also for the here and now. His kingdom is here, *now. Shalom* is for today. We don't have to go away on a retreat to experience it or shut ourselves off from humanity while we get ourselves together. The apostle John wrote, "The Word [Jesus] became flesh and blood and moved into the neighborhood" (John 1:14 MSG). I love that! The beauty of God's grace, given to us in

Jesus, is that it is perfectly at home in the messiness of our everyday lives.

Although we will not experience its fullness until we reach heaven, we can begin to reclaim *shalom* now. If you feel that you can't even see all of the pieces of your life, let alone put them together, it's okay. Keep your eyes on Jesus. He is *shalom* itself. When you accept His invitation and follow His lead, you can take consistent steps on the road that leads to wholeness, well-being, and ultimately peace. And that's how you begin to allow God to set the tempo for your life, to walk with Him in rhythms of grace. That is *shalom*, everything as it was meant to be.

As you'll discover next, one of the most natural places we begin to find our rhythm is in creating Sabbath zones in our lives.

For Reflection

1. What are your go-to solutions or behaviors when things start to spiral out of control? Which of these things are working for you right now? Which ones aren't?

2. If you could experience *shalom* in the context of your daily life, what would it look like — at home, at work, in your relationships, when you are alone, etc.?

3. What do you sense the Holy Spirit might be saying to you about *shalom* wholeness?

28 SepT 2016

Chapter 3

Sabbath: God's Metronome

The Sabbath was made to meet the needs of people,
and not people to meet the requirements of the Sabbath.
Mark 2:27 NLT

When I was around nine years old, my mother decided I should take piano lessons. It made sense because I loved music and had been singing solos in church since the age of four. But singing was something I did for fun, and tiresome lessons and hours of practice did not sound like fun. Nonetheless, I dutifully attended my piano lessons. Much to my surprise, I actually enjoyed it. I really liked my teacher and I loved being able to play and sing at the same time.

One of the things I did not like, however, was the metronome —the little device that marked time with military precision to make sure I played to the right rhythm. Each time I sat down to play a piece I had been practicing, my teacher started the metronome. I tried to play according to its measured timing, but I almost never did it right. Sticking to the prescribed rhythm was hard! My teacher would gently correct me, "Kerri, that was very well done. You hit all the right notes. But your timing was off. You have to play in rhythm. If you don't, the song will not sound the way it is meant to sound—the way it was written by the composer." I began to hate that little metronome. It was like a bossy babysitter—no fun at all.

I didn't understand why rhythm was so important. Even at nine years old, I could tell that although my rhythm was off in a few places, it was a far cry from ruining the song. And why did it even matter that I was playing it differently than the composer intended? It wasn't like he was turning over in his grave when I butchered his masterpiece. What I didn't realize at the time was that playing according to the composer's intended rhythm is not so much for the times when musicians play their instruments alone, but for the times they play with other musicians or an orchestra. It's the thread that ties all the individual pieces of the symphony into one, beautifully cohesive piece.

Rhythm, not melody, is what grounds the music and makes it possible for musicians to make music together. Of course, it's usually the melody we love—that's what gets stuck in our heads, what we sing in the shower, and what sometimes moves us to tears. But without rhythm, the notes that make up the melody would be bouncing all over the place. In an orchestra, the keys, the strings, and the wind instruments would have no reference point for when to play the notes. Instead of playing in a unified symphony, an orchestra without rhythm would be a chaotic jumble of individual interpretations of the score.

Sabbath is God's metronome, marking out a weekly rhythm of rest and renewal. It is our reference point for knowing how to plan and live our lives. Without the Sabbath, our lives are a jumbled mess of individual events; with Sabbath, they can be a beautiful balance of labor and rest.

Yet, just as I once found it difficult to play the notes of my music to the beat of the metronome, we can find it difficult to let the rhythm of Sabbath rest set the pace for our lives. So many other things seem like better, more comfortable metronomes. Shouldn't our educational and career goals set the pace? Our kids' activities? The church calendar? Those things are important and have a legitimate place in our lives, but they are the notes of the melody—the unique song of our individual lives—not its foundational rhythm. Unless God's rhythm of rest sets the baseline beat, we will miss the composer's intent for our lives—and His intent is *shalom*. If we want to reclaim *shalom*, we have to let God's metronome of Sabbath rest set the baseline beat of our life's rhythm.

29 Sept 2016

The Rhythm of Rest

A regular, recurring interval of rest and renewal should occupy a sacred and nonnegotiable place in our lives. God created the Sabbath as a dedicated space for rest, not as something we get to do if and when we finish all of our work. Without a regular and recurring space for rest in our lives, we might have a lot of movement going on, but we probably won't be living in a rhythm of grace.

You see, not all movement has rhythm. Some movement is just that ... movement. There may be lots of motion happening, but none of it is connected to any kind of intentional pattern. Anything that has rhythm has measured, regular, and recurring patterns. That's what rhythm is. Whether we are talking about the melody of a song, the steps of a dance, or even the items on a personal schedule, rhythm is created by beats that repeat in a pattern.

I didn't understand for a long time about my own life, so I developed a habit of swinging between the extremes of feast or

famine: full-on work or full-on rest. This habit started inno-
cently enough and with good intentions. Most of the work I do is
project-based, which means I can set my own hours and schedule
as long as I meet my deadlines. When my children were in grade
school, I scheduled intense work seasons followed by a few weeks
of rest. I chose to do this so I could spend extended periods of time
focusing on my kids and family. Even though there were times
I was incredibly stressed out and distracted, I could endure them
because I knew a long season of rest and fun was coming.

For a time—a long time—it worked fine, but it wasn't sustainable. I would work super hard and push myself to the limits
(famine). Then I would drop everything down to a near stop and
rest (feast). These cycles naturally coincided with our children's
school year. Summers and holidays were laid back and low key
while the spring and fall semesters were intense on every front.
As time went on, though, summers and holidays started to take on
the same level of intensity that once belonged only to the spring
and fall.

We began to travel more. We went back to our hometown
for holidays and attended conferences during the summers. Then
our children became involved in sports camps and mission trips.
Because the spring and fall were so crammed, I began to push
long-range projects into the summer months and holiday seasons. Slowly but surely, the down time we so desperately needed
got shorter and shorter, and eventually it disappeared altogether.
We were always working, but just in different settings. All this
time, I truly believed I had a rhythm to my life. I called it a sea-
sonal rhythm. Yet it wasn't actually a rhythm. There was a lot of
movement and activity, but it lacked the essential characteristics
of rhythm: measured, regular, recurring patterns.

What I know now that I didn't know then was that God has
a rhythm of rest and renewal in place in the form of Sabbath rest.

Thousands of years ago, when He commanded the Israelites to observe the Sabbath each week, God set a baseline beat of rest and renewal that would set the pace for their lives—and for ours.

Sabbath's Hidden Message

For the ancient Israelites, keeping the Sabbath meant that every single person in the nation, and even the animals, would cease from all work for a twenty-four hour period:

> Observe the Sabbath day, to keep it holy, as the LORD your God commanded you. Six days you shall labor and do all your work, but the seventh day is a Sabbath to the LORD your God. On it you shall not do any work, you or your son or your daughter or your male servant or your female servant, or your ox or your donkey or any of your livestock, or the sojourner who is within your gates, that your male servant and your female servant may rest as well as you. You shall remember that you were a slave in the land of Egypt, and the LORD your God brought you out from there with a mighty hand and an outstretched arm. Therefore the LORD your God commanded you to keep the Sabbath day. (Deuteronomy 5:12–15 ESV)

The Sabbath began at sundown on Friday and ended at sundown on Saturday. There were special Sabbath practices and commandments (called *mitzvahs*) that each family observed. They ate Sabbath meals together and recited Sabbath prayers. Observing the Sabbath was a commandment—a law—but the Sabbath itself was intended to be a gift. Each week, as work took a toll on bodies and souls, the Israelites could look forward to the rhythm of Sabbath and the guaranteed gift of rest. What might look like a restriction on the surface actually communicates a hidden truth: *You are free. Free to rest, free to regather the scattered pieces of your life, and free to relish the goodness of God.*

Like a telegraph echoing across the ages, God has sent us a divine message encoded in the commandment to observe Sabbath rest. The Sabbath reminded the Hebrew people of an important event in their history: the day they were freed from slavery in Egypt. The phrase God most frequently uses to describe himself in the books of the law is, "I am the LORD your God, who brought you out of Egypt." Sabbath was a weekly reminder of their liberation.

Why was it important that God's people be reminded of their liberation? Well, imagine that your whole life, from the time you could walk to the time you were laid in your grave, every single day consisted of almost nothing but work. Miraculously, you and your family are then suddenly rescued from this life of oppression. As part of the new laws of your emerging nation, God Himself commands that you take a day off every single week to rest and enjoy Him and the people you love. What a revolutionary inversion of every single thing you had ever believed to be true about the world and about your place in it! The Sabbath made a declaration week in and week out to the people of Israel. It wrote this message over and over again across their lives: *You are no longer slaves. You are free.*

What does it mean to be free? Maybe it would be easier to answer the question, "What does it mean *not* to be free?" Masters rule the lives of their slaves—when they eat, sleep, bathe, go to work, and end their work. For slaves, all the rhythms of life are dictated by the master's will. The same is true for us—we are servants of whatever gets the first and best of our time.

We might not think of ourselves as being in bondage, but is there anything that more clearly signifies freedom from the systems and values of this world than the ability to cease working and to rest? If we can't rest, if we won't rest, then are we truly free?

I live in America, a country described as "the land of the free and the home of the brave." But sometimes I wonder if what we call freedom is the kind of freedom God envisions for His people. God speaks about spiritual freedom. This means that when we accept Christ as our Lord and Savior, we are free to live for Him, not for the things of this world.

Jesus said, "No one can serve two masters. For you will hate one and love the other; you will be devoted to one and despise the other. You cannot serve both God and money" (Matthew 6:24 NLT). When Jesus chose a master to pit against God in this statement, He chose money. He could have chosen lust or murder, but He didn't—He chose what the King James Bible refers to as "mammon." Mammon came to represent the system of the entire world, which is driven by one thing: profit. For our own time, we might add productivity and the drive to maximize our limited resources at all costs—even if our soul suffers, and it surely does.

Mammon—the materialistic system of this world—is the ultimate oppressor, and its origins are as ancient as the earth itself. Back in Eden, when Adam and Eve fell and the image of *shalom* was shattered, chaos entered the world once again (cf. Genesis 1:2). Work became a yoke of oppression instead of a joyful expression of purpose, for without it there would be no provision. God's last words to Adam before he left Eden sound almost like a funeral dirge: "Cursed is the ground because of you; in pain you shall eat of it all the days of your life; thorns and thistles it shall bring forth for you; and you shall eat the plants of the field. By the sweat of your face you shall eat bread, till you return to the ground" (Genesis 3:17–19 ESV).

Since that day, the world has marched to the beat of profit and productivity. The gods of profit and productivity pervade the fabric of this world to such an extent that we swim in their influence every day and don't even realize how thoroughly drenched we are in their values. Even though, as individuals, we might not be driven by greed, we live in a time and culture that is. Perhaps without even realizing it, we move in response to its music and the tempo of our lives is set by its rhythm.

The system of this world is opposed to grace. Grace frees us from the burden of proving our worth by our works, but Mammon values us *only* according to the measure of our work. Grace says, "God's grace is sufficient." Mammon says, "It all depends on you—provision will only come through work, toil, and the sweat of your brow." When *shalom* was the rhythm of the world, the song of earth matched the song of heaven, but now they clash like clanging cymbals. The sweat of Adam's brow—his anxiety, toil, and worry—set the baseline beat of our world outside the gates of Eden, and the beat still goes on.

Mammon might be the ultimate oppressor, but God is the ultimate liberator. In giving the Israelites the Sabbath, God gave *shalom* a place to take up residence. When Jesus said, "Come to me, all you who are weary and burdened, and I will give you rest" (Matthew 11:28), I can't help but believe that He meant to call the Sabbath rest to the minds of those listening. He gives *shalom* a place to take up residence in our lives, and by His grace it remains. Do you see? The Sabbath is not just an ancient ritual but a present-day gift for those whom God loves and holds dear. It's a holy moment in time that declares He will never leave us nor forsake us. Because His grace is sufficient for us, we no longer toil and work by the sweat of our brows in order to prove our worth by our works. Our worth is wrapped up in Him.

Establish Your Sabbath Zone

No matter what kind of schedule you have, establishing what I call a Sabbath Zone in your weekly rhythm is a foundational component for living in rhythms of grace. This applies just as much to stay-at-home parents as it does to those who work full-time outside the home. Maybe you have chosen the wonderful, rewarding life of staying at home with your children, but you have committed them to so many activities that you feel like you are working two full-time jobs. Or perhaps you are retired and busy volunteering or traveling to see friends and family, and you have forgotten that a regular time for rest is necessary for you to continue to respond to the needs of others. Regardless of your tasks and responsibilities in this season of life, a regular experience of Sabbath rest is essential.

Sabbath was intended to be a day to replenish our souls by filling them with good things. It's one of the most important ways to experience joy in God and to stay spiritually strong. My idea of filling my soul with good things often means relaxing with a good book—and not necessarily the Bible or a devotional book. For others, "good things" might include going for a walk on the beach, spending time with a friend, writing in a journal, or engaging in a creative pursuit such as photography or painting. Perhaps simply having a blank space on your calendar and doing nothing is your idea of filling your soul with good things. Whatever way you replenish your soul, the aim is to experience the special kind of joy that comes from enjoying a day with and for God in the posture of rest.

Here are some suggestions for ways you can create a Sabbath zone, which is simply a regular and recurring rhythm of rest in your week.

Make Sabbath a mind-set. If you are just now beginning to realize that you have minimized the importance of rest, this is a good place to start. Begin by reflecting on your current approach to rest. For example:

- How do you tend to view people who prioritize rest? Do you consider them lazy, self-indulgent, privileged, sensible, wise? What does your view of others reveal about your attitudes toward rest overall?

- What thoughts or emotions come to mind when you think about making decisions to prioritize rest in your life?

- To what degree, if any, does your need for rest factor into the decisions you make about how you spend your time each week?

- Overall, would you say that rest is something you wish you could experience more in the course of your week but rarely do, or is it something you routinely plan for and enjoy?

- What factors either keep you from planning for and experiencing rest, or make it possible for you to do so?

Observe Sabbath as a weekly day of rest. This is my approach to creating a Sabbath zone. Fridays are my day off. When I come home from work on Thursday evenings, I make a conscious decision to mentally and emotionally disconnect from work. I take a few minutes in the car and do a mental checklist of what I completed during that week, and also what I need to do the next week. I might make some notes on my phone. I then take a brief overview of the weekend, put my phone in my purse, and say a prayer, offering up the next twenty-four hours to God and asking him to give me rest. When I walk through the door of my home, I leave the week behind and make a conscious decision to be fully present in the moment. I stop thinking about the past or future. I focus completely on the here and now.

My full attention is given to my husband and my children. I don't take calls or check email. I don't plan next week's work or mentally rehash the details of the past week. For the twenty-four hours in my Sabbath zone, all that matters is *the present.* I focus only on *what is.* When I first began to do this, it became sadly obvious how many precious "now" moments I wasted by being preoccupied with the future or the past.

I have heard it said by many people that eternity is the absence of time, but the more I practice the weekly rhythm of Sabbath, the less I believe that to be true. I have started to wonder if perhaps eternity is not the absence of time, but the absence of decay. The ways we mark time's passing have little, if anything, to do with time itself. We do not get old because time passes. We get old because our bodies are subject to aging and decay. Buildings do not crumble into ruins because of time, but because the fabric of our world is temporal and passing. Time stands outside of the material world, and each week in my Sabbath Zone, time stands still. For just a little while, it is like breathing the air of eternity —a place where decay is banished.

Observe Sabbath using Jewish customs. In their book *Sitting at the Feet of Rabbi Jesus*, authors Ann Spangler and Lois Tverberg offer suggestions on how Christians can practice Sabbath observance by using Jewish customs.[2] Practices might include things such as the following:

- Aligning the time of your Sabbath zone with the Jewish Shabbat (Sabbath), which begins Friday at sundown and concludes at sundown on Saturday.

- Beginning your Sabbath observance with a blessing from Scripture and the lighting of candles.

- Speaking blessings over your family. In the Jewish custom, the father speaks a special blessing over his wife and children. In addition, there are special blessings for wine and food, ritual hand washings, and blessings following the Friday evening meal.

Many are blessed by celebrating the Sabbath according to Jewish tradition. It can be a wonderful thing to participate in and can add a rich layer of understanding to your reading of the Scriptures on the subject of Sabbath.

However you choose to establish your Sabbath zone, it doesn't have to happen perfectly every week. Is anything in our lives perfect? Don't get hung up on that. Jesus said that the Sabbath was for people—for us—not the other way around (Mark 2:27 NLT). If a weekly observance doesn't work for you right now, try starting with once or twice a month and see where God leads. Grace will cover you as you find the Sabbath rhythm for your life.

God's Gift for Our Peace

We might believe that working harder than everyone else is the way to the life we want, but that is just the siren song of this world's system. The system of this world is not designed to produce freedom, wholeness, or rest. It doesn't matter how hard you work, how long you toil, or how much you sweat, because this machine, this system, was not made to contain *shalom*; it was made to produce profit, and that is all it will ever be good for.

I encourage you to commit your heart to wholeness and to begin by committing yourself to Sabbath rest. Let's be believers who declare with our lives that we are free from the system of this world. Let's choose to routinely devote space in our weeks for some form of Sabbath rest, a day to mend our tattered lives and reclaim wholeness.

When we trust in God's grace enough to rest from our labor, we are freed from the tyranny of attaching our security to our work—or to anything else we might want to control. Tracey R. Rich, a blogger who writes about Orthodox Jewish life, describes the gift of freedom within the Sabbath:

> Shabbat frees us from our weekday concerns, from our dead-lines and schedules and commitments. During the week, we are slaves to our jobs, to our creditors, to our need to provide

for ourselves, but on Shabbat; we are freed from these concerns, as much as our ancestors were freed from slavery in Egypt.[3]

Six days a week we strain our ears to hear the beat of heaven's drum above the clamor and chaos of this world, but on the Sabbath, we tune our ears to one sound alone. In the gift of Sabbath rest God invites us to enter a slice of eternity, where, just for now, the song of heaven and the song of earth are the same — note for note, measure for measure, beat for beat.

For Reflection

1. What is setting the baseline beat for your life right now? How do you feel about letting a rhythm of rest set the baseline beat instead?

2. The message of the Sabbath is: *You are free.* What does that message mean to you personally? In what areas of your life do you most need to experience freedom?

3. What is your mind-set about Sabbath? In what ways do you value, or fail to value, rest?

4. What do you sense the Holy Spirit might be saying to you about the Sabbath?

Chapter 4

28 Sept 2016

Grace:
The Yoke of Christ

For my yoke is easy to bear,
and the burden I give you is light.
Matthew 11:30 NLT

I learned how to snow ski fairly late in life. I was thirty-eight when I made my first attempt to conquer the slopes. When my husband initially brought up the idea of snow skiing as a possible family vacation, I was resistant. I couldn't imagine why anyone would want to go somewhere freezing cold and spend all day exercising (which is my least favorite thing on the planet to do). I finally gave in to his pleading to "just try it once," and, much to my surprise, I loved it!

Gliding down the slopes felt like flying. The grip of gravity seemed to loosen a bit as I leaned into the terrain. The best part of it was that I was having so much fun that I didn't even realize I was working out. Skiing burns tons of calories—and that means, of course, carbs every day and dessert every night. Ski vacations quickly became one of the highlights of my year.

But there was one drawback—the boots! They hurt like crazy. When I was being fitted for my first pair at the rental shop, the young man who was helping me warned, "Now you need to remember, these are not supposed to be comfortable. They will be a little constricting, especially at first." Boy, was that an understatement. They were downright painful, but I pressed on because I believed they were supposed to hurt at least a little bit.

Over the next five years, we continued to make our annual family trip to the slopes, but each year I skied less and less. Wearing the boots eventually became so painful that I spent several hours each day in the rental shop just trying to get a fit comfortable enough to go down the slopes a few times without stopping. I adjusted the straps and tried all sorts of custom inserts. Nothing helped. The clerks at the store tried their best, but the boots continued to hurt me. Each year I was met with the same explanation: they aren't supposed to be comfortable. By the end of our fifth trip, I sadly resigned myself to the possibility that I might not be able to continue skiing.

In our sixth year, I determined to give the ski boots one last go-around. As I had done so many times before with many different clerks, I began to explain the issues I had with my boots. Essentially, I have hobbit feet: wide and flat with large calves. (Thankfully, however, I don't have all that hair.) I told him I had never been able to find a boot that fit properly, and this was my last try before I gave up skiing for good.

"I know the boots are supposed to be a little uncomfortable," I said, "but I don't think this is what they are supposed to feel like. It's beyond discomfort. Sometimes the pain literally brings me to tears. I end up sitting on the side of the slopes to loosen my boots just so I can make it down. Skiing's not fun anymore. I just don't know what to do."

The clerk looked at my feet and measured for size. "There is a brand of boots made especially for people who have wide feet and larger calves," he said. "It's not an uncommon problem at all. Let me bring some out for you to try on."

From the moment I put my feet into these new boots I could feel the difference. For one thing, my blood could circulate. That's always a plus. My calves weren't squeezed and pinched; my feet weren't wedged into Chinese foot-binding proportions. I was so overjoyed that I almost laughed out loud. I would be able to ski again—and I did! That week I spent the whole day every day on the slopes without stopping. It was the most fun I'd had in years.

What I learned from the boot saga is this: fit is everything. It can make you or break you. When my boots fit properly, they helped me progress smoothly and efficiently down the slopes. They were supportive, not constrictive. Snug, not suffocating. The old, poorly fitted boots had worked against me. I felt the pain and pressure of every turn and each stop. The old boots were an obstacle rather than an aid. But not the new boots. The right fit released me to focus on my purpose for being there in the first place—skiing!

Skiing is supposed to be challenging and exerting. It's a work-out! But it's also supposed to be fun. There were times when I needed to work hard to concentrate on turning at just the right angle or shifting my weight at just the right time. There were times I needed to go gently down the familiar green and easier blue slopes, and there were times to push myself on the tougher blue slopes (no black slopes for me, thank you very much). The right gear made finding my rhythm on the slopes easy. When I needed to push my limits, the right gear supported and steadied me.

So why all this talk about skiing and gear? Because it's a good metaphor to talk about the life God calls us to. Life, like skiing, is supposed to be a mixture of work and fun. Finding *shalom* is not at odds with working hard. Regardless of whether or not we get paid, we all have work to do in this life. Each person's work is unique because our circumstances, experiences, personalities, gifts, interests, and passions are unique. Yet there is at least one thing we all have in common: our life's work is also a gift of worship to God. That's why the apostle Paul writes, "Take your everyday, ordinary life—your sleeping, eating, going-to-work, and walking-around life—and place it before God as an offering" (Romans 12:1 MSG).

God does not separate Himself from the day-to-day tasks and moments that make up our life's work. Such work *is* our work for God, even if it's something as seemingly ordinary as changing diapers a hundred times, negotiating a business deal, or teaching unruly students. Doing our daily tasks with joy and excellence is an act of worship. Our work, and how we do it, matters to God.

There will always be a certain amount of tension between our work in life and times of communion and rest with the Father, but we can find balance between the two by making the decision to fall into step with Christ and move to His rhythm. How do we do that? We take on His yoke.

The Perfect Fit

In Jesus' day, farmers used a yoke—a kind of collar—to link two oxen to each other. The yoke was then attached to some other object, such as a plow. Linked by the yoke, the two oxen could then work together, pulling whatever burden was attached to the yoke. Jesus applies this image to our life with Him:

> Come to me, all who labor and are heavy laden, and I will give you rest. Take my yoke upon you, and learn from me, for I am gentle and lowly in heart, and you will find rest for your souls. For my yoke is easy, and my burden is light. (Matthew 11:28–30 ESV)

Don't you think it's a little bit strange that Jesus' idea of getting us to rest in Him involves putting on a yoke? A yoke was not created for rest; it was created for work. It literally has nothing to do with rest at all. When Jesus invited the weary and heavy laden to come to Him and find rest, we would expect Him to say something like, *Take off that yoke you're wearing—you don't need it anymore! Doesn't that feel great? Now run ... be free!* But Jesus' solution for yoke-weariness was not to cast off the yoke entirely; it was to yoke ourselves to Him, to walk in step with Him. This is a different kind of yoke, one perfectly fitted to support and aid us in fulfilling His purpose for our lives. That doesn't mean being yoked to Christ will always be comfortable, but—like well-fitting ski boots—it's not supposed to crush us either.

Farmers used to train young oxen to plow by partnering them with stronger and more mature oxen. The job of the younger ox was simply to follow in the same direction and keep pace with the teacher ox. The older ox pulled most of the weight and understood the commands of the plow driver. As long as the young ox followed the older ox, everything was fine. But if the younger ox decided to speed up or lag behind, the work became much more difficult. Only by keeping pace with the older ox could the younger ox complete the day's work without collapsing from exhaustion.

When we are yoked to Christ, He carries most of the weight. Being yoked with Him means that we are living in a way that allows us rest because we are under His covering of grace. So what do I mean by "grace"? It's a huge word that is a kind of catchall for everything amazing about God. There are endless ways we could talk about grace, but we're going to focus on two aspects of it. Grace is God's undeserved favor that puts us in right relationship with Him, and grace is the power God gives that enables us to live the life He's called us to.

The heavy-laden people Jesus spoke to did not know grace. Instead, they were yoked to a complex system of Jewish regulations referred to as "the law." Obeying the law as perfectly as they could was how they stayed in right relationship with God and made sure that the work they were doing for Him was acceptable. The reason Jesus didn't tell His listeners to throw off the yoke completely is because they still had work to do—and as long as we are alive, we too will always have work to do. Work is a good thing. We were created for purpose, and that purpose often finds expression through our daily tasks. A life without work is not possible, nor is it desirable. So the question is not, "Will you work?" but "*How* will you work?" How will you pull the burden of your life's work along?

The people in Jesus' day were using the yoke of the law to pull their life and everything in it along. In some ways, they were like me with my calendar grid, trying to impose order on their outer lives in order to solve an inner problem—and it left them "tired, worn out, and burned out on religion." The yoke of grace Jesus offered was contrary to the yoke of the law. It was a move from depending on one's own efforts and ability to depending on God's grace and power.

Today, most of us don't suffer under the yoke of the law like Jesus' listeners did, but we have other yokes. For us, it's not so much a choice between the yoke of grace or the yoke of the law, but between the yoke of grace and the yoke of performance. When we believe that being productive in our life's work depends completely on our own performance, the weight of laboring under that yoke can be crushing. For example, we want to be the best parents possible, so we look for the ideal parenting methods. How our kids turn out is the measure of our parenting success (we think), so we stress out about every little thing they do wrong or might do wrong. If they don't turn out "right," everyone will know we were failures. Or perhaps we want to be the best at our jobs, so we take on more and more because we are afraid that saying no means we might fall behind, lose some of our perks, or be overlooked for the next raise or promotion. Eventually, the overwhelming demands on our limited time and energies render us incapable of hearing the voice of God because we don't even have time to stop and listen.

When we pull the burdens of life by the yoke of our own performance, then performance sets the pace. We race faster and faster, trying to outdo our last personal best or to measure up to the expectations of others. But when we take on the yoke of Christ and let Him lead, He determines the pace, and we find that His grace makes up what we are lacking in our performance.

The apostle Paul gives us a great example of the yoke of grace in action. Paul had pleaded three times for the Lord to remove what he called "a thorn in my flesh" (2 Corinthians 12:7). We don't know what the thorn was. Some say it was a painful health issue, while others say it may have been a temptation he consistently struggled against. No matter what it was, we can be sure that Paul saw it as a torment and a hindrance to his life's work. But when he asked the Lord to remove it, the Lord replied, "My grace is sufficient for you, for my power is made perfect in weakness" (2 Corinthians 12:9).

Paul realized that because God's grace was enough, his performance didn't have to be perfect. His weaknesses, sufferings, hardships, persecution—anything that worked against him to trip him up—provided an opportunity for the grace of God to be shown for how powerful it really is. Paul came to a place where he was so dependent on the grace of God that he could say, "For the sake of Christ, then, I am content with weaknesses, insults, hardships, persecutions, and calamities. For when I am weak, then I am strong" (2 Corinthians 12:10 ESV). Imagine not only enduring weaknesses, but being content with them—accepting them and trusting that our weaknesses are an occasion for the display of God's grace and power!

God's wonderful grace is just enough for you and for me. His grace releases us from the pressures of perfect performance. When we admit that we are not perfect and never can be, we affirm our belief that God is perfect and everything about Him—His work, timing, strength, provision—is perfect as well. So what does this mean in practical terms? Well, if you're married, let's say you've been preoccupied with a work or a personal issue and feel guilty about not being more attentive to your husband. Or maybe as a parent, you feel like you have failed because you can't afford to pay for your children's college education. As a friend, perhaps you feel guilty that you haven't "been there" enough. Right now, I encourage you to *stop* and immediately exit the guilt train. Wherever you are lacking, God's grace can and will cover you. He designed you knowing that you wouldn't be perfect—He never had that expectation for you. So why do you have that expectation for yourself?

The yoke of Christ is perfectly fitted to support and aid us in fulfilling His purpose for our lives. It's not always comfortable, but that's not the point. It is always what I need for the path He wants me to walk. Under the yoke of grace, I don't evaluate my worth by how many items are checked off on my to-do list. Under the yoke of grace, I do not measure my value against anyone's expectations—not even my own! Nor am I full of discontent as I hurry toward a more perfect future version of myself. Under the yoke of grace, I rest content with where I am right here, right now, weaknesses and all—as long as I am walking close to Jesus.

Three Questions to Help You Step into Rhythms of Grace

How can you tell if you are under the yoke of Christ and in step with Him, or if the yoke of another master is around your neck? Remember my experience with the ski boots? The same principle applies here. When the fit is right, the journey—not the gear—is the focal point. When we labor under Christ's yoke, we're not focused on the yoke. Instead, we are able to enjoy the work and the journey.

But what about when we don't? Sometimes we're wearing the wrong yoke. Other times, we're wearing it for the wrong reasons. When I'm feeling overwhelmed with ministry tasks and life commitments, there are three questions I ask myself to get back into step with the rhythms of grace.

QUESTION 1: Who Put This Yoke on Me?

Jesus already told us what His yoke feels like: easy and light. If your yoke is not easy and light, Jesus might not be the one who put it on you. Remember how the intense pain from my poorly fitted ski boots almost caused me to give up skiing? One of the things that kept me from pressing harder for a solution to my problem was the mistaken belief that my boots were *supposed to hurt*. More experienced skiers kept telling me the boots were supposed to be uncomfortable. Some even said, "Well, some people are not cut out for skiing. Maybe you're one of those people." I started to believe them.

It wasn't until I got boots that fit correctly that I realized that the term *uncomfortable* was subject to a wide range of interpretation. Uncomfortable is a far cry from agonizing and debilitating. The truth is, no one else could wear my boots with me. No one else could know exactly how I felt. They could only relate what I was describing to their own experience. I had to trust my intuition, and it was telling me that my uncomfortable and their uncomfortable were not the same thing.

For many years, I labored under the yoke of performance and all the unrealistic expectations that came with it. I had this whole idea of what was expected of a pastor's wife, or to be more precise, what I thought people expected of me. Especially in the early years of planting the church, I felt so guilty if I didn't attend every Pampered Chef party and baby shower. I thought that was what a pastor's wife was supposed to do, so I tried as hard as I could to meet those (false) expectations. I had to prove that I could fill the role well. Even as I began to set healthy boundaries and be more intentional about my schedule, I still labored under the guilt and fear that I wasn't measuring up.

Can you see how a performance mentality was at the root of my desire to meet expectations? I had to perform in order to prove my worth and be accepted. The sad thing was that the expectations I thought people had of me were mostly manufactured in my own mind. I was the one who thought pastors' wives should attend every event and respond to every need. For the most part, our church members extended way more grace to me than I extended to myself. Now that I am under the yoke of grace, I realize that I don't have anything to prove. I will make mistakes and disappoint people, but that's not because I'm a failure as the wife of a pastor. It's because I'm a human being. I am accepted and covered by God's grace—weaknesses, failures, and all. And the good news is that we only have to strive to please one person —Jesus. If I am earnestly trying to obey His commands, then everything else will fall into alignment.

QUESTION 2: What Is Motivating Me?

When we find ourselves doing life at an unhealthy pace, we have to consider our motivation. Why do we continue to push ourselves at a pace we know is unhealthy? When I burned out, I had to ask myself this question, and I came to realize that even though I was doing a lot of the right things, I was doing them for the wrong reasons. I don't know what that might look like in your life, but for me it meant jumping into ministry opportunities at times when my presence would have added more value at home. Or forcing myself to sit dutifully through every minute of my daughter's three-day dance competition because I didn't want to be "that mom" who put her career ahead of her children.

There's nothing wrong with doing ministry and attending dance competitions, but I was doing these things at the wrong pace because I was doing them for the wrong reasons. I was doing them because I thought I had to; I didn't realize I actually had options. I didn't allow myself to question why (motives) or how (pace) I was doing things. And the "why" and the "how" are just as important as the "what" (actions). The right things done for the wrong reasons or at the wrong pace are still the wrong things.

As I sit here writing these pages, I've got the same responsibilities as I had a year ago. I did not cut anything in particular out of my schedule. The big difference is I am no longer doing it with a sense of external obligation—the expectation that doing this or that somehow validates me as a person, or qualifies me as a good mother, or any of those other sorts of false motivations. Jesus' opinion of me and my accomplishments is the only opinion that will matter in the end. My work is my worship. He is the only one I am trying to please. His yoke is easy, and His burden is light.

QUESTION 3: Who Am I Trying to Please?

It's natural to want people to be happy with us, but we have to let go of the delusion that pleasing everyone all the time is even possible. Jesus was perfect, and even He couldn't please everyone all the time (Luke 7:33−34). He knew that the only person He needed to please was the Father. He was so committed to pleasing God that He did only what He saw His Father doing and spoke only the words He heard His Father speaking (John 5:19; 12:49). But pleasing God doesn't necessarily mean that we can, in turn, please everybody else. For example, God might be leading you to take up a new challenge, but some members of your family aren't supportive. He might be inviting you to volunteer more — or less — of your time, yet your friends don't agree. People might not understand what God is saying to you, but you must follow His lead anyway.

We must accept that we will sometimes be misunderstood. Jesus was misunderstood, and He didn't go around to each person to make sure they understood "His heart." I'm all for making peace with others, but even Jesus could not be at peace with everyone. There will be people who will disagree with you. Sometimes they will misunderstand you and misjudge you. When that happens, keep your focus on pleasing one person — Christ — and let the fruit of your life speak for itself.

As we learn to listen to God's voice and move according to God's rhythm, we will discover the ways that we can find rest and wholeness in Him. By taking on Christ's yoke of grace, we make it a habit to submit our plans and our ways to Him; we affirm our belief that He is wiser and stronger and can guide us at a pace we could never guide ourselves.

One of the ways He does this is by helping us see that almost everything in life can be defined as either a pacesetter or a peace stealer. Next, we'll learn more about these setters and stealers, discover how to move at the pace God has for us, and learn how to eliminate things that compromise our ability to find *shalom* and live a Sabbath lifestyle.

For Reflection

1. How would you describe the "yoke" you're laboring under right now? In what ways do you feel in step or out of step with Christ?

2. As you were reading through the three questions about the yoke you're carrying (pages 65–68), what thoughts came to mind about your own life?

3. In what situation(s) might you need to cast off the yoke of another master and take on the yoke of grace?

4. What do you sense the Holy Spirit might be saying to you about grace and being yoked to Christ?

Part 2

28 SEPT 2016
20 OCT 2016

PACESETTERS AND PEACE STEALERS

SABBATH REST SHOULD SET THE BASELINE BEAT OF OUR LIFE'S rhythm, but there are some additional things that impact the pace or tempo of our lives in varying degrees. I call these key areas of life "pacesetters." They include things like work, relationships, physical health, and spiritual vitality.

In the chapters that follow, we'll take a closer look at how we can keep each of these pacesetters in a healthy state by taking a proactive rather than a reactive approach. If we fail to be proactive, these pacesetters will take on a negative momentum of their own, keeping us from living in *shalom* and experiencing the wholeness and peace we desire.

Chapter 5

What Are Pacesetters and Peace Stealers?

Therefore, since we are surrounded by so great a cloud of witnesses, let us also lay aside every weight, and sin which clings so closely, and let us run with endurance the race that is set before us, looking to Jesus, the founder and perfecter of our faith, who for the joy that was set before him endured the cross, despising the shame, and is seated at the right hand of the throne of God.

Hebrews 12:1–2 ESV

One of the world's most grueling ultramarathons takes place in Australia every year. This 543.7-mile (875-kilometer) endurance race from Sydney to Melbourne takes six to seven days to complete, and it is normally attempted only by world-class athletes under age thirty. These expert runners train for years for this race and are sponsored by huge, multinational sports companies. Even among this gathering of elite and skilled runners, some still do not cross the finish line. The race is just that grueling.

In 1983, Cliff Young, a sixty-one-year-old potato farmer from Beech Forest, Victoria, showed up at the start of this race. To everyone's shock, Cliff didn't come to the race as a spectator. He came to run. He picked up his race number and walked to the starting line. While the other runners stood there stretching and warming up in their corporate-backed, state-of-the-art running gear, Cliff Young shuffled up to the line in his work boots and overalls with holes cut in the knees for ventilation. Oh, and without his teeth since, he said, they rattled when he ran.

When the race started, the professional athletes bolted off the line and left Cliff behind as he shuffled along at a turtle's pace. He didn't even seem to know how to run properly. His feet barely left the ground as he shuffled along in his rubber boots. Naturally, Cliff Young turned into an overnight legend just for entering the race. No one seriously expected him to win, but they found him enormously entertaining even as they were also concerned for his well-being.

When television reporters asked Cliff Young what kind of runner he was and if he thought he had a chance at winning the race, he answered, "Yes, I can. See, I grew up on a farm where we couldn't afford horses or tractors, and the whole time I was growing up, whenever the storms would roll in, I'd have to go out and round up the sheep. We had two thousand sheep on two thousand acres. Sometimes I would have to run those sheep for two or three days. It took a long time, but I'd always catch them. I believe I can run this race." When Cliff was asked about his tactics for the rest of the race, his answer surprised everyone even further. He planned to pace himself so that he would be able to finish the race without sleeping.

The standard approach to completing this monumental test of endurance successfully was to run for eighteen hours each day and sleep for six hours. That's what the other runners did, but not Cliff

Young. With the morning of the second day came another surprise. Cliff Young had not stopped running during the night. He had continued shuffling along at his awkwardly slow and steady pace all night long. In the first forty-eight hours, he covered two hundred miles. As each night passed, he moved closer and closer to the front of the pack. While the other athletes ran harder and slept longer, Cliff Young continued on day after day at an almost laughably slow pace. But by pacing himself that way he was able to conserve so much energy that he only needed to sleep for one hour each night, giving him an additional five hours longer to run than his competitors.

By the final night of the race, Cliff Young had surpassed all of the younger, world-class athletes. In a win that truly deserves to be described as legendary, he crossed the finish line in Melbourne almost ten hours ahead of the next runner. In five days, fourteen hours and thirty-five minutes he had covered 875 kilometers, running the equivalent of almost four marathons a day. His time broke the standing race record by more than two days and changed the way the race was run from then on. Modern competitors in the Sydney to Melbourne race do not sleep. Now in order to win the race, runners must run all through the night and all day, just like Cliff Young.

The legend of Cliff Young is not well-known outside of Australia, but it should be. It is a remarkable, modern-day version of the tortoise and the hare and a striking example of how important pace is when it comes to winning or losing a long-distance race. Obviously, everything was working against Cliff—his age, his attire, and his lack of professional training. Nobody took him seriously because he was the most unlikely person to win.

Maybe you have had "Cliff Young" moments in your life. There may have been times when you felt that everything was working against you and that you just didn't have the right gear or qualifications. Maybe right now you are running a race in life it seems that nobody—including yourself—believes you can actually win. Just like Cliff Young, it is important that you pace yourself for the road ahead. When you learn the art of pacing, you will be able not only to stay in the race, but also to finish strong.

Pacesetter Tensions

There are certain things that, by their very nature, set the pace of our lives. They are such big parts of our day-to-day existence that they have an undeniable impact on the tempo of our race in this life. I call them pacesetters. We don't all have the exact same pacesetters, but most of us do have a few in common. These include work, relationships, physical health, and spiritual vitality. We'll focus on each of these in the chapters that follow, but the principles and guidelines we'll cover also apply to any other pacesetters that are unique to your life.

Perhaps the ways in which these common pacesetters impact the tempo of your life is one of the main reasons you picked up this book. You might be wondering how to slow down the tempo imposed on your life by work so you could have more space in your life for family, friends—or even God. Maybe the pace of things has made it difficult to slow down and really connect. Or possibly you want to make time for a healthier lifestyle because you're experiencing some undesirable consequences of neglecting this area of your life. You know you need to make time for exercise, but you're not sure how you will fit it into a weekly schedule that is already crammed packed with too much to do. Or perhaps you have been out of work for a while and are now reentering the work place. Maybe you are wrestling with the fear that adding work into your schedule will negatively impact your family.

Work, family, and health. Most of us struggle to balance these things in our lives. We might see work as something tha petes with family, or we might feel forced to choose betwee taking care of our family's needs and our own needs. When we can't honor one area of life without sacrificing another, the result is tension. Here are some pretty revealing definitions of the word "tension":

- the act of stretching or the state of being stretched or strained
- mental or emotional strain; stress
- intense, suppressed suspense, anxiety, or excitement
- a strained relationship between individuals, groups, nations, etc.
- a balanced relationship between strongly opposing elements[4]

Do any of these definitions resonate with you? The feeling of being "stretched too thin" is a common way I hear women describe the tension of competing demands and responsibilities placed on them. Or maybe you feel like your relationships are strained because events and commitments in your life sometimes require you to choose one person over another.

Imagine that the two opposing forces that are causing the most strain in your life are two people, each holding opposite ends of a long rope. Now imagine that each person begins to pull on the rope at the same time. What happens? The rope gets tight. It gets tense. Right at the point when the rope reaches the farthest it can stretch, there is a "snap" at the center of the rope. This is the point of tension. It's where the power of the two opposing forces meets. If the rope doesn't break, then whoever pulls the strongest wins the tug of war.

Our natural response to tension is to balance it or to resolve it by letting go. When we try to balance the opposing forces in our

nter point on that rope. We feel the "snap"
:es pulling against each other, and we bear
esponsibility of balancing the tension caused
don't snap first (and there's a good chance we
ventually fall over toward the side that exerts the
it's the only way to resolve the tension and relieve
ourselv.   e strain it causes.

Neither balancing nor resolving the tension between opposing forces produces the peace and fulfillment we're looking for. Here's why. Work, relationships, and health are not optional pieces of life. They are essential components. If we fall over on the side of family and neglect work, we might miss out on the joy that comes from pushing our limits to create, build, and produce something meaningful with our lives. But if we fall over on the side of work to the neglect of family, we move in the opposite direction and all the things we accomplish through our work will have no meaning in the long run.

We all have to do work of some kind. Work is just what has to get done, whether that is knocking out quarterly reports, turning in a term paper, organizing a birthday party, or cleaning the kitchen before you do the last load of laundry at midnight. We know that the things that constitute our work are not more important than our family and friends, but the reality remains that we must get them done. And the truth is, we want to do them well. We don't want to leave out family, but do we really want a whole life where we never really accomplish anything? I would bet that most of us don't.

Even in the world of Eden, a world of perfect *shalom*, there was the work of exercising dominion and subduing the earth (Genesis 1:28; 2:15) — that's a pretty big job description. I believe that there will also be work in heaven. The descriptions of heaven in the Bible speak of the nations coming and going, and of elders that rule. In other places we are told that believers who endure will reign with Christ (2 Timothy 2:12). Those things sound like work to me. The difference between work in Eden or heaven and work on earth is that in Eden and heaven, work, relationships, and health are not in opposition to each other. They are all just pieces of the bigger picture on the box top—the picture of *shalom*.

The reason we feel tension between the various aspects of our lives is because we are trying to balance things that were created to exist in harmony with each other, not in opposition. In a world characterized by *shalom,* work is not at odds with relationships, relationships are not at odds with health, and rest is not at odds with productivity. The fragmenting that comes from putting these areas of life at odds with each other is not what God intended for us in the beginning—and it's not what He intends for us now. His intent was, is, and will be *shalom.* The key is not finding the perfect work/life balance, or giving in and falling over to one side or the other. The answer is seeing all that we do as worship. Worship resolves the tension because it acknowledges that the million things we have to accomplish are ultimately under the care of God. He's in control, knows our capacities, and will see us through. When we have that mind-set up front, it allows us to approach each of these essential pacesetters with a sense of wholeness, balance, and health.

You may have noticed that I did not include your schedule in the list of common pacesetters. That's because when your schedule is functioning properly, it actually does not function as a pacesetter. I know that when most people think of the pace or tempo of their lives, the first thing that usually pops into their heads is a picture of their calendar or their to-do lists. But calendars and project lists do not set the pace of your life; they are a reflection of what you allow to set the pace of your life. They are simply systems that support goals, vessels that contain what you value. For that reason, they are important, and we'll talk more about how to create a schedule that honors rhythms of grace in chapter 10.

The important thing to remember for now is that a schedule is not meant to be a performance grid that we need to measure up to. Instead, it is a servant of our greater purpose, which is keeping pace with God's divine tempo and arranging the pieces of our lives according to the vision of *shalom*. We get what we schedule, so we need to be careful about what goes on the agenda. It's an easy trap, but if we end up focusing on productivity and not *shalom*, our tasks will become taskmasters. But when we learn what brings wholeness in the things that are pacesetters for us, we will also know how to build a schedule that is designed to contain it.

Reactive or Proactive?

When it comes to our pacesetters, the most important shift we need to make is moving from a reactive to a proactive way of living. If we are not proactive about pacing our lives, eventually we will fall into a reactive mode in which we simply respond without thinking to everything life tosses our way. That's when a pacesetter becomes a peace stealer. For example, I absolutely love everything about the Christmas season. However, if I'm not proactive in planning for it, my joy and excitement can quickly be replaced by stress, worry, and anxiety. For me, being proactive includes buying presents early, making travel arrangements early, and getting a jump on our family Christmas cards. Otherwise, if all of these things creep up on me at the last minute, I won't be running at a pace that will enable me to enjoy the holidays.

When we approach life in a reactive posture, it's challenging to experience peace. Constantly having to react to whatever life throws our way forces most of us to assume a defensive or protective posture. Suddenly, our time isn't devoted to accomplishing the things that will enrich our lives but to battling the things that steal our joy. That's when we end up running behind, running ragged, and running scared that we'll disappoint our families, our friends, our small groups, our bosses, or any one of the nineteen people who need something from us *right now.*

In contrast, when we are proactive, we initiate change rather than react to it. The prefix "pro" means "advancing or projecting forward or outward." When we assume a proactive posture in life, we advance toward what we want rather than living defensively and reacting in opposition to what we don't want. We take new ground in areas that are important to us, and we initiate the activities and changes we need to make in order to have the life and peace we long for.

To live in a proactive way, we have to know where we want to go. For this to happen, we have to make space in our lives to first identify what's important to us and then to plan for it. As people who lead busy lives, sitting down with a calendar and a journal just to think might seem like a luxury we can't afford. I used to feel positively guilty about taking time to dream and plan, as if I weren't really accomplishing anything. But the truth is, if I don't consistently set aside time to do so, I soon become reactive and other people's agendas quickly begin to shape the course of my life.

Of course, I want to leave room to respond to unexpected needs, but that is a different thing than simply reacting to every unforeseen event. Identifying what's most important to me during a given season of life and then planning for it is the only hope I have for creating the margin I need to navigate life and respond to the unexpected in a peaceable way. When I fail to be proactive in any of the areas that are pacesetters, they become peace stealers.

Most of us probably already know all too well what peace stealers are and how they affect us. If you're feeling burned out and overwhelmed, you don't need me to identify your pain points. But I do want to acknowledge that feeling and use it to encourage you.

You already have the most important part of the answer. Apply the three principles we covered in part 1 — *Shalom*, Sabbath, and Grace. Those foundational rhythms come into play exactly when we feel worst about our circumstances. To move from a reactive to a proactive posture, there is nothing more important than declaring a Sabbath zone and resting in God for a day. That's doubly true when you're feeling weary and depleted. Even a moment of rest can be restorative. God wants you to have a reprieve.

Then, as you look at your work, don't let the length of the list or the difficulty of the tasks dictate your attitude. Take the first thing and offer it to God. I'm not saying this is easy, but notice your heart. Notice your emotions. Now try to approach your task prayerfully. Make the errands, the expense report, the after-school program, the conference call, whatever — make them a prayer. Something will shift. It's when we start incorporating rest — Sabbath rest — into our days that we begin to experience *shalom* in the middle of life's storms.

With that background in mind, let's now take a closer look at four common pacesetters and how we can prevent them from turning into peace stealers.

——————— *For Reflection* ———————

1. In what ways, if any, do you relate to the story of Cliff Young?

2. What two or three things are causing the most tension in your life at the moment? In what ways are you responding proactively? In what ways are you responding reactively?

3. The chapter identifies four common pacesetters. Are there additional pacesetters that are unique to your life? If so, what are they?

4. What do you sense the Holy Spirit might be saying to you about your pacesetters?

Chapter 6

Your Work

Therefore do not worry about tomorrow, for tomorrow will
worry about itself. Each day has enough trouble of its own.

Matthew 6:34

I clicked "send" on my last email of the day. After two weeks out
of the office, the backlog of work had really piled up; but after
one good day in front of my computer, I had managed to empty
my inbox and get back up to speed. What a relief! I looked at the
time and discovered it was only 4:30 in the afternoon. *Wow. Not*
only did I catch up, I finished early! I can head home now and beat the
traffic. Just as I stood up to pack my briefcase, I noticed a pile of
papers I needed to go through by the end of the week. It was only
Tuesday, so I had time. Lying on top of the pile was the brochure
for SHINE, our church's annual women's conference. *Great! I have*
been wanting to see this for weeks—I can't wait to see how it came out. I
know it needs to go to print soon. I will just take a peek, but I won't work
on it till tomorrow.

That's what I told myself, but that isn't what happened. "Just
a peek" turned into to "just a few text edits," which turned into

some rewrites. The more I looked at the pages, the more I noticed little things here and there that could be improved. By the time I looked up from my "peek" it was 5:30, the height of the traffic rush. If I left for home right then, I would spend an extra twenty minutes at a standstill on the highway. *May as well spend those twenty minutes getting work done till the traffic dies down. Then ... I wonder if Elaine is still here.* Elaine is our lead graphic artist. She is both incredibly creative and sensitive to deadlines. I knew she would be as happy about getting ahead as I was.

I walked into Elaine's office just as she was about to shut down her computer for the day.

"Elaine, you did an amazing job on the brochure!" I said, "I love it! And I wanted to show you a few minor changes we need to make now so I don't hold up the project."

Maybe Elaine's heart sank with disappointment at being even further delayed when she had already stayed late, but she didn't show it. She just smiled and said, "Sure! I was hoping to talk to you tomorrow, but this is as good a time as any."

By the time we finished going over a "few minor changes," it was 6:15 — forty-five minutes had passed. I looked down at my phone and saw a barrage of texts and voicemails from my family:

Kaylan: *When are you getting home?*
Stovall: *What's for dinner?*
Three calls.
Three voicemails.
Stovall: *Should I pick something up?*
Babysitter: *Will you still be home by 6:30? Don't forget, this is the night of my mom's birthday party. Just a friendly reminder.* ☺

And there it was. A day that was perfectly finished at 4:30 turned into overtime for Elaine and me because I couldn't resist the lure of *just one more thing.* I couldn't say, "That's enough for today."

On the way home, I mentally rehearsed the events at the end of my day over and over again. I had already been out of town for several days and came straight into a full weekend at church. I really wanted this night to be a time for our family to reconnect around the dinner table. I had even planned out a special menu and made sure Stovall and the kids would be home, and then ... what happened? Where was the breakdown? I was so frustrated with the way things had turned out.

Why couldn't I just have been satisfied when I completed my work for the day? Why do I always feel I need to use every extra minute to get ahead? Why don't I ever feel satisfied with the work I get done in a day? How is it that I never feel as if I have accomplished enough? When is enough really enough?

What makes it so hard for us to be satisfied with what we accomplish in a day? I tend to overestimate what I can accomplish and overload my calendar. Once I am committed to something, I am too embarrassed to admit to myself or to others that I have taken on too much. Then there's the fear of letting people down. Of course, not all of the reasons we overdo it at work are based on negative emotions. We might just love what we do and find it exciting and energizing. That's what prompted me to take "just a peek" at the SHINE brochure. I had a nagging suspicion that once I picked it up I might not be able to put it down, but in my excitement to see the mock-up of the final design I ignored my intuition.

The Work/Rest Rhythm

A big part of our life's rhythms are set by how we balance work and rest. How would you describe your work/rest rhythm? Is it a deliberate and dependable routine that, while not exactly exciting, at least doesn't interfere with the rest of your life? Would you describe it as a good mix between a challenging, upbeat tempo and a measured, comfortable stride? Or perhaps you feel like there is no rhythm at all, that you have a lot of chaotic movement but nothing that resembles a sustainable work/rest rhythm. A sustainable work/rest rhythm that leads to wholeness is one that leaves us with something left at the end of each day. The key to establishing such a rhythm is learning how to be content and satisfied with one day's work, but the challenging thing is that determining what constitutes "one day's work" is becoming increasingly difficult. Why?

The answer is that the way we work has changed dramatically even since the turn of the century. When I began my first career as a high school teacher in 1992, cell phones weren't common. When I entered the classroom at 8:00 a.m., I left the rest of the world behind. I had one hour during each day to use for lesson planning and whatever other needs I might have. During that hour, I could check messages and return phone calls. The Internet didn't even make it into homes in my southern hometown until a few years after that, and I didn't get my first computer until 1998. Until then, faxing was how the movers and shakers got things done. The technological landscape of the world created natural boundaries between work and the rest of life in a way that's difficult to imagine in our current landscape of nonstop connectedness that blurs the lines between our personal and professional lives.

The smartphone revolution has made it nearly impossible to disconnect from work. That comes with advantages and disadvantages, which are, interestingly enough, the same. We can work from anywhere and everywhere—and we do. When you turn on your phone first thing in the morning, the temptation to start working before you even get dressed for the day can be surprisingly difficult to resist. Your inbox icon explodes with email notifications that you want to ignore, but then again you want to have an idea of what you might be facing today. So you give in and open up the first one.

The carpool mom canceled and wants to know if you can fill in for her. Your boss sent an email at midnight (again) and called an emergency meeting first thing this morning. A text message pops up from your friend saying, "I just found out Amy has lice. I know she and Chloe have been playing together a lot this week. So sorry—just found out." *Great. Now I have to fumigate my house and pick lice nits out of Chloe's hair today ... and I guess the boys', too.* All of that has just gotten thrown at you through a two-by-four-inch screen in less than two minutes while you are still brushing your teeth.

Home and work are entangled now for better or for worse, and the mash-up is irreversible. Natural boundaries between those spheres no longer exist for most people, and so the burden falls on us to create them. There comes a time when we have to look at the work we have completed and say, "That's good enough for today." But when will that time come? At what point will we be able to look at the number of projects we've completed, the cabinets we've cleaned out, or the phone calls and emails we've returned, and say, "Tomorrow, I'll pick it up again, but for today my work is complete"? There is no cut-and-dried biblical rule that tells us how many hours a day to work and how many hours to rest, but God does model a daily work/rest rhythm for us in the Genesis account of creation.

When God rested from His creation work, all the components for life on earth were in place. Yet it is certainly conceivable that God could have continued creating and done more had He wanted to. The earth was not yet fully populated; God left that job to Adam and Eve. There was room for more fish in the sea and animals on the land, but God put the mission to multiply into their hands. He could have invented who knows how many more species or subspecies of every living creature, but He didn't. He looked at what He had accomplished and said, "This is good!" Then He stopped and rested from His labor.

And notice this: God didn't stop only after He had completed the whole project of creation. He stopped each and every day when He was finished with that day's work. We can find God's project list for creation week in the first two chapters of Genesis:

Day 1: Create light from darkness; name each.

Day 2: Separate waters in heaven from waters of earth; name each.

Day 3: Separate water from dry land; make plants.

Day 4: Create sun, moon, and stars; mark out the seasons.

Day 5: Make sea animals and birds; give instructions for multiplying.

Day 6: Make land animals and humankind; give instructions for multiplying. Hand off stewardship responsibilities to Adam and Eve.

Day 7: Relax and enjoy!

Each day had a rhythm of work and rest that was based, not on how much God could do, but on how much was enough or appropriate for that day. If God, who could have kept working on and on without ever getting tired, stopped working when there were still things He could have done, then doesn't it seem obvious that we, too, must stop working when we have done enough for one day?

Choosing to be satisfied with one day's work simply means doing what is appropriate for each day—no more, no less. It means resisting the urge to do more just because you can or because you have extra energy. It also means not quitting or giving up just because you are frustrated or because you believe no one will notice. The appropriate amount of work differs from day to day. Some days, twelve hours might be required, but on other days six hours of work is enough. The work/rest rhythm ebbs and flows at different tempos through every season of life. With God's guidance, we are free to move at the right pace for each time and season.

Along with finding the right rhythm for the different times and seasons of our work, there are different contexts and approaches for what we do. We'll look at those next.

Home vs. Work

There is no fool-proof formula for managing the demands of work life and home life, but I've discovered that there are two basic ways most people approach setting the rhythm of their work-home dance: they are either work-focused or home-focused. I should probably mention a disclaimer here, that not everyone has work outside the home — at least, work for pay. Sometimes people who do volunteer work or are involved in nonwork activities can have just as much of a problem with balance. The descriptions that follow have in mind someone who is working outside the home, but they could also apply to those who volunteer or do not have a paying job outside the home.

Moreover, there are five distinct styles people tend to fall into when they seek to balance the demands of work and home life. As you read the descriptions that follow, notice which seem to describe you best. Don't worry, this is not a test! There are no right or wrong answers. But knowing where you tend to focus and what your style is will help you to better understand and navigate the demands of home and work.

The Work-Focused Person

A work-focused person gains a lot of satisfaction from being successful in the workplace. This person is usually an outstanding performer because success at work makes her feel valued and successful as a person. While work-focused people are typically driven, efficient, and productive, they have two key challenges that can sabotage a healthy work/life rhythm.

First, the work-focused person can easily feel like a failure when her work performance doesn't meet the highest possible standards. Because her identity is strongly linked to her work, her self-worth has a tendency to go up or down in relationship to her success in the workplace. Second, the work-focused person can feel tense and distracted in the home environment where the standards of successful performance are not clear and where relational connection, not productivity, is the goal. She might even try to create standard measures of performance so that it resembles the more comfortable world of work, and she feels more confident that she is doing her home job well.

Being a work-focused person is not a bad thing. Maybe you weren't expecting me to say that, but I truly do believe it. Just knowing and acknowledging this fact about yourself is freeing. Having a work focus is not always a trait that is celebrated or affirmed in women, especially in Christian women. Work-focused women tend to feel guilty about it and may try to downplay their work success or how energized they are by their work because they don't want to be perceived as overly ambitious, or worse, as neglecting their families for the sake of their careers. As a result, they may not be fully aware of how strongly they identify with their work, which leaves them with blind spots when it comes to balancing the demands of work and home with wisdom.

If you are a work-focused person, you can establish some

simple practices to help you better navigate between work and home. Here are a few examples:

Give yourself wrap-up time. Set a thirty-minute reminder at the office to alert you that it's time to start wrapping up your day. After that point, don't open up any new projects that you can't complete before you go home. Begin to wrap up your day before it's time to walk out the door. This applies even if you work from home—maybe especially if you work from home. The proximity to family can be deceptive. It's easy to think you're present when you're really still giving your time to other tasks.

Give yourself transition time. This is something I practice regularly. Just before I get home at the end of the day, I stop in the parking lot of a small park in my neighborhood. I give myself ten minutes of quiet in the car with the phone on silent and the radio off. I take that time to close out my day emotionally, mentally, and spiritually. I celebrate my high points, release my low points to God, and give any unresolved issues to Him. Those ten minutes become my transition time and help me to avoid bringing home the emotional and mental burdens of my work.

Give yourself a phone-free zone. Instead of keeping your phone (or other electronics) with you throughout the evening, make the decision either to turn it off completely or to give yourself scheduled phone-free zones and phone-check times. For example, put your phone away for the first two to three hours after you get home, and check it only after the kitchen is clean following dinner. Make a decision not to look at your phone (or other electronics) after a certain hour, and then not to look at it before a certain time in the morning (like after you get dressed for work).

Our work does not define us, but our approach to work defines the quality of everything outside our work. If we are not mindful of our approach, an important pacesetter in our life can become a peace stealer.

The Home-Focused Person

The primary source of value and satisfaction for a home-focused person is tied to the well-being of her home environment. While doing her job well is important to her, her performance in this sphere isn't what's most important to her. Just as with the work-focused person, the home-focused person has a unique set of challenges that can sabotage a healthy work/life rhythm.

The home-focused person can easily let any anxieties related to home and family spill over into her work life. If she gets into an argument with her husband before coming into work, or if she knows one of her children is facing a challenge at school, her work is likely to suffer because she is preoccupied with personal concerns. She might also feel overly responsible for the feelings and burdens of the people in her family and take on more than she can handle in order to relieve their stress—which causes her stress to spike even more. It's easy to see how this person can feel overwhelmed and out of control!

If you are a home-focused person you can establish some simple practices to help you navigate between work and home. Some examples are:

Give yourself a clean start to the day. Avoid initiating any serious or sensitive discussions with family members before you leave for the day. Save these kinds of discussions for when you have enough time to resolve them if they venture into conflict. Similarly, avoid escalating any existing conflict if at all possible. If your children push your buttons or do something that could escalate into an all-out war, let it go for the moment and make a note to address it later.

Give yourself transition time. Just as the work-focused person needs to transition from work to home at the end of the day, the home-focused person needs to transition from home to work at the beginning of the day. Before you walk into the workplace, entrust your family life burdens to God so you can put your focus where it needs to be while you are at work. Keep a notebook and pen in your car or purse. Before you leave the house or just when you arrive in the parking lot at work, write down the unresolved issues and home burdens that could distract you. Briefly pray and acknowledge that God is carrying them for you. Choose to trust Him while you are at work by imagining Him hold those burdens for you. That concrete image might help you focus on His ability to carry your burdens

Give yourself set times to check in at home. Knowing that these times are coming regularly throughout the day will free you up to concentrate on work. When you find yourself distracted or preoccupied with concerns at home, remind yourself that you will check in at the scheduled time. When your thoughts begin to drift off into worry, try saying out loud, "I am going to check in at home at 2:30." This will reinforce your decision to stay focused and remind you that you set this timeline and you are capable of sticking to it.

Finding the balance between home and work is never easy, but it's essential if we're going to have wholeness — *shalom* — in our lives. One helpful tool is identifying the way we best manage home and work tasks throughout the day. There are five different styles that we'll look at now.

Five Styles of Balancing Work and Personal Life

Another factor that impacts our work/life balance is the degree to which we combine or separate the tasks associated with work and those associated with our personal life. How much do we allow work to interrupt home and home to interrupt work? As you read through the five styles that follow, pay attention to which one describes you best right now.

Mergers blend work and person
throughout the day. They ⸢
time, and home to interrup
with business calls, texts, o
even on vacation. While at
to help a school-age child ⸢
social event.

Now take a m
the two kinds
and home.
focused
cut ⸢

Separators keep work and pers⸢
separated into defined bloc
on work, and at home they focus on family life. If they
have to attend to a personal matter during the workday,
they usually schedule it at the beginning or end of the day
or use break time or lunch hour. Separators have clearly
established boundaries that protect both work time and
home time.

Work elevators allow work-related calls, texts, or emails to
interrupt home life or even vacations. They regularly use
technology to keep them connected to work no matter
where they are. They have clear boundaries protecting
work time, but tend to lack similar boundaries to protect
home time.

Home elevators allow home to interrupt work. At work, they
use technology to stay connected with home and family.
For example, they may use work time to email or phone
a child or to schedule a doctor's appointment. They have
boundaries protecting home time, but they allow work
time to be interrupted.

Rotators switch back and forth between cycles of integrating
home and work followed by periods of separating them.
The rotator tends to compensate for the losses of intense
work seasons (missed personal or family events) by
devoting herself to intense home seasons to catch up with
all that has piled up on the personal front.[5]

oment to reflect on what you've just read about
of focus and the five styles for balancing work
Which ones best describe you? Are you more home-
or more work-focused? Are you a separator, with clear-
boundaries between work and home, or are you a merger,
ending everything in one big happy mush? Just having clarity
about your tendencies is a huge step toward better navigating your
advantages and challenges and fitting them together with greater
ease and less tension.

Running on Empty

Whatever your focus and style, the most important thing you can
do is remember that your divine tempo — a rhythm that leads to
wholeness — should not leave you feeling empty and dry at the
end of each day. It will leave you with a little left over. If you ran
out of gas on the highway, you wouldn't pat yourself on the back
for using up every last drop of fuel, saying, "I am a really dedicated driver. I drove until there was nothing left to give." On the
contrary you would be kicking yourself for not leaving enough
reserves in the tank to reach your destination, and then make it to
the next gas station to fill up again. When it comes to your bank
account, you don't congratulate yourself for spending every last
cent each month. The goal is to have a little something left over, a
reserve. We don't treat any other resources as if the goal is to spend
or use them until they run out, but we do this with our own time
and energy thinking that somehow this proves how spiritual we
are. But it doesn't prove anything except how much we under-
value the only things we can't actually put a price on.

It's not that we should never work long hours to get things
done. There are occasionally times for that, and I have them

myself. But I don't routinely live like that anymore. For me, a forty-hour work week really is a good amount, and that includes working from home after hours. I might work as many as sixty hours a week when a crucial project deadline must be met. But even then, for short periods of time and followed by a day or two off to recuperate. To think that you can make a habit of working a sixty- to eighty-hour week without crashing and burning or creating havoc elsewhere is delusional.

Work is a good thing. We are beings created with a drive to be productive and to make an impact for good, and our work is a huge part of that. But a life devoted primarily or solely to work is a poor substitute for truly living. The writer of Ecclesiastes summed it up this way:

> What exactly do people get out of all their work and all the stresses they put themselves through here under the sun? For every day is filled with pain and every job has its own problems, and there are nights when the mind doesn't stop and rest. And once again, this is fleeting. There is nothing better than for people to eat and drink and to see the good in their hard work. These beautiful gifts, I realized, too, come from God's hand. (Ecclesiastes 2:22–24, The Voice)

When we find ourselves at "enough" for the day with extra time and energy left over, we are just where we should be. Let's decide that we will receive it as the gift that it truly is. Each day has a measure of work and worry—and also a measure of grace. Tomorrow's work will be waiting for you, and so will tomorrow's grace. Today's measure of grace got you through today, and tomorrow's measure of grace will get you through tomorrow. So use today's grace for today, and don't worry about trying to shoulder tomorrow's burdens with it as well. Each day has enough trouble—and grace—of its own.

For Reflection

1. How do you feel at the end of each day? Are you tempted to stay a little later and get ahead? Or is it easy for you to flip off the "work switch" and close down for the day?

2. Which type of focus do you tend to lean toward? Are you more work-focused of home-focused?

3. Which type of balancing style do you prefer? Are you a merger, a separator, a work elevator, a home elevator, or a mix of styles?

4. What do you sense the Holy Spirit might be saying to you about your work?

Chapte

Your Relati

And let us consider how we may spur one another on toward love and good deeds, not giving up meeting together, as some are in the habit of doing, but encouraging one another—and all the more as you see the Day approaching.

Hebrews 10:24–25

Remember the T-Mobile plan "Fave Five"? It was a phone plan that allowed you to choose the five people you talked to the most and put them on a list of favorites so that you could have unlimited interaction with them without chipping away at your minutes or allotted text messages. These five people had unlimited access to you, and you had unlimited access to them all day, from anywhere in the United States via text or phone—they were part of your Fave Five!

It's nice to be part of a group of someone's favorites, but it hurts to realize you didn't make the cut. Imagine how uncomfortable this conversation would be:

> "Hey, guess what! I just put you in my Fave Five. Now we can text as much as we want!"

owed by the awkward response, "Sorry, but
ot in my Fave Five. ☹. Nothing personal ... My
n *made* me put her in, *sooo* ..."

on't have any evidence to prove it, but I wouldn't be sur-
sed if T-Mobile dropped this plan at least partly because of
people complaining about the havoc these little exchanges
unleashed on their friendships. Who wants to know they didn't
make the Fave Five list? It's like musical chairs on cell phones.
Eventually, someone is going to be left out.

Obviously, not everyone can be in your Fave Five, which is
your inner circle of relationships. Some people should be included,
and some people shouldn't be included. It's not a matter of whom
you love, but of who has a legitimate claim to place relational
demands on you.

Our closest relationships have an especially strong impact on
the rhythms of our lives. It doesn't matter if we want them to
or not; they just do. Close relationships are pacesetters. There
are certain relationships that have the right to claim that role in
our lives and some that don't. It's crucial not to confuse the two,
because the people who make up your inner circle will—and
should—set the pace for your life.

To whom do you owe the greatest responsibility? Through
whom will you leave the greatest legacy? Because your inner circle
sets the pace of your life, you need to make sure the right people
are in that position. Wholeness in the area of relationships is having
the right people, in the right circle, and investing in them at the
right level.

Your Circle of Relationships

Imagine you are the center dot in a circle diagram.

The concentric circles around that dot represent your relationships in decreasing levels of intimacy. Think of these circles like real estate. There is only so much space available in each ring of the circle. The closer someone is to you—the center of the circle —the greater the impact they will have on you (in both positive and negative ways). You will be impacted by:

- their strengths and their weaknesses
- their needs and their contributions
- their function and their dysfunction

And all of these same things inside of you will impact them.

Here is how I currently label the circles in my relational diagram:

My circles include family, friends, my domain of influence relationships, and acquaintances. Your circles may look different than mine. For example, you might label your circles family, church friends, coworkers, and community. And it's also true that some categories might change depending on the season and circumstances of your life. For example, if you were to retire, coworkers might be replaced by neighbors or new friends.

However you label your circles, it's important to remember that we are looking at relationships through the lenses of wholeness, not through the lenses of time management. As we consider what it might look like to proactively take steps toward relational wholeness, we must first make sure that the people in our lives are in the right circles.

In a real way, those closest to us shape our lives and play a significant part in charting its course. So it's especially important to know who gets into that first circle because those relationships will have the greatest impact on us. These are the people who have a legitimate claim to be in our Fave Five. Let's start out with who should be in the inner circle.

The Inner Circle

Your family — your spouse, children, parents, and siblings — belong in your inner circle. These people have a legitimate claim to be pacesetters in your life. For some, that makes perfect sense. *Of course they belong there. Where else would they go?* I think we might all agree to this in principle, but what does that principle look like in real life? Here's a personal example.

By placing my family in the inner circle, I affirm that they have the right to expect me to arrange my time and resources so that they are the primary beneficiaries. My children have the right to expect that I will consider them first before making decisions that impact them. My husband has the right to expect that I will talk to him when I consider my dreams and plans for the future. My parents have the right to expect a place of honor in my world above other people. My sister has the right to expect the same. It's perfectly legitimate for them to expect me to take visiting them into account when I make my annual travel plans. My parents and in-laws have a right to expect my involvement in their care as they age and need extra help. They have a right to expect these things from me, and I have the right to expect the same from them. Their claim to be in my inner circle is a legitimate one.

So what does that mean? It means that when they place these legitimate demands on the relationship, I don't get resentful and sullen. I make room in my life to respond to the needs that have to be met in order to keep these relationships healthy, loving, and mutually beneficial. If we don't prioritize the relationships that have a legitimate claim to be pacesetters, then those that don't have a legitimate claim will rise up to fill the vacuum. The people in our lives who should be in our inner circle are then displaced; they no longer retain the role of pacesetters. Someone else sets the pace, and they get moved to an outer circle. This is how we can end up being out of touch and disconnected from the people we love without realizing it. Instead of our spouse setting the pace, work sets the pace; instead of our kids setting the pace, our opportunities do; instead of our parents setting the pace, our social calendar sets the pace.

If you think I am saying that our families should be the primary relational pacesetters in our lives, you're right. That's exactly what I am saying. I don't mean that we should give up all of our hopes and dreams, all of our ambitions and our individuality, to attend and document every soccer practice. But sometimes I wonder if we have become so self-focused that we have forgotten what it really means to be a family. Not all relationships are created equal. Some relationships are more important than others—and they *should* be more important than others. Family relationships are those relationships.

Even so, for some people family members are not the ones who fill up the inner circle. Perhaps they live far away from their families, or there has been so much strain and hurt over the years that healthy family relationships are not possible. For these people, good friends may take up the space normally occupied by family. But everyone needs to have someone in that space—people who are like family to you. That means people who not only support you, but who can depend on you for support as well. However, even when we have the right people in the inner circle, the demands of daily life sometimes shift our focus away from what's most important to us.

I follow a funny little Twitter account called @honesttoddler, which presents the daily interactions between parent and child from a toddler's point of view. One day the toddler tweeted: "For nine months they dreamed about what my face would look like. Now they're watching YouTube videos trying to run out the clock until bedtime."

I laughed when I read this because I remember thinking the same thing when our children were preschoolers. One night we were all sitting on the sofa watching some kids' movie or another to bridge the gap from dinnertime to bedtime. I looked over and observed Kaylan watching the movie, Stovie playing with his action figures, and Annabelle doing a headstand on the sofa next to Stovall, who was dead asleep! I thought, *We spent years dreaming of what it would be like to have a family, but we never dreamed it would be like this!*

My dreams of being a mom consisted of making handmade birthday invitations and having long, meaningful family devotions around the dinner table, which would be set with homemade organic meals. I never thought "family night" would mean eating a deli chicken and watching *Barney's Great Adventure* for the fifth time while counting down the minutes till 8:00 p.m. when we could put the kids to bed. It seemed like the day flew by in a flurry of activity without us really even listening to or looking at each other for more than a couple of minutes. Our bodies were inhabiting the same space, but our minds and hearts hadn't really met all day.

There are bound to be days like this when you're a parent. After all, there is a real house to manage, a job to maintain, and dinner to cook. You reach the end of your rope some days and feel like you have nothing left to give. Sometimes you just want to crash into bed and hope for a better day tomorrow. But when every day starts to be an exercise in "counting down the minutes," we are missing an important truth. The tomorrow we envision is actually in the minutes we are counting down today. Here's the most important part: the only harvest we will ever reap will be the fruit of the seeds we sow. If our minutes are the seeds and our tomorrows are the harvest, how can we hope to reap what we have not planted?

It doesn't take much to get our focus off of being connected to the most important people in our world, but neither does it take that much effort to return our focus to them. Making the people we love a daily priority doesn't mean we have to sit down to a three-course meal every single night, play family games for hours by the fire, or have theologically rich family devotions. Here are two things you can do every day to make an intentional investment in your family. These are simple changes and easy to implement.

For starters, *prioritize conversation that goes beyond the logistics*: homework, doctor's appointments, dinner plans, chore lists. All of these things are about function but not necessarily about connection. Conversation that goes beyond logistics means finding out what was interesting about all those things and why; what was exciting that day; what was happy or sad; what made someone spit out their drink with laughter. Ask about the day's high and low points, and listen without offering correction or making a judgment. This is a small thing that would change the atmosphere in many homes and impact the relational dynamic of many families in a positive way. Going beyond logistics means getting past information and finding what our souls say about the day.

Next, *give affirmation to each member of your family*. Never underestimate the power of telling someone what you see in them that makes them special, or to recognize something you appreciate about them. Everyone wants to know they are seen, known, and loved. For example, pick out one thing to praise about each person. Maybe your son or daughter has been struggling with math; let them know that they're more valuable than their test scores — and when they finally get it, let them know that you are proud. Maybe your husband has been working extra hard for the family — affirm him. Let him know he's appreciated. The praise should be tailored for each person. Finding something unique to affirm does wonders for your family—and for you.

Daily investment in our families doesn't have to be complicated or time intensive. It just needs to be done consistently and in a way that is focused and unrushed. Our moments today are our tomorrows in seed form—and we can sow them with intentionality.

Friends

After family, the next people in our inner circle are our closest friends. These are the people we invest in on a daily or weekly basis. Even if we do not live near them or cannot see them on a regular basis, they are the people with whom we have deep and lasting attachments. I do not live in the same state as most of my family, but I still consider them part of my inner circle. I am intentional about talking with and visiting them regularly.

Not many friends can take this place in our lives. Since our families have a right to take a pretty big chunk of our inner circle real estate, most of us typically have limited space for friendships at this level of commitment. You might think that sounds unloving or elitist, but it's not. It's just realistic. Time, like money, can be spent or it can be invested. When we spend money, we trade it for goods or services: food, shoes, a haircut, a vacation. When we invest money, what we want to get in return is more money. We want the value of our investment to increase and multiply over time. The most stable investments mature slowly. Spending is about getting something now; investing is about getting something later. If we spend everything we have and never make investments, we will have nothing for the future. But if we stop spending and determine that we will only invest, we will have nothing now. We need to do a little of both to enjoy life.

The same goes for our relationships. Some friendships are investment relationships and some are spending relationships. Investment relationships are the ones to which you devote substantial time and energy. Spending relationships are more for simple fun and joy.

Investment relationships. Together with the people in these relationships, you are investing time with a mutual goal—to lean on, glean from, enjoy, and create connections with each other. Most of my investment relationships are my friends on our church staff. We naturally spend a lot of time together because we have work in common. But beyond that, I truly enjoy being around these friends. When I'm tired and want to unwind, they are the first people I call. When I need someone to talk to who understands the tension in balancing work and family demands, I reach out to them. When I have a funny story to tell and I know only a few people will get it—these are my go-to friends. I have other investment relationships with people who are not on staff, and we stay in touch as much as possible. But friendships that are built around shared work and purpose have endured the wear and tear of the daily grind for years—these are my investment relationships. They benefit me in the present, but most importantly, these are the people with whom I have a history and to whom I am committed for the long haul.

Spending relationships. Not every relationship can be an investment relationship, and that's okay. Spending relationships are friendships that are characterized by common interests and having fun together. You can relax, be yourself, and just enjoy each other's company. You might not have the most in-depth conversations with these friends, but that's okay. Not every friendship is meant to have the same dynamic or serve the same purpose. Just enjoy these friendships for what they are—but right-size the time you devote to them. If you have to make a choice, more often than not your investment relationships should take priority over your spending relationships.

The Outer Circles

What about all of the other layers of the relational circle? Our coworkers, acquaintances, and neighbors? Relationships in areas where we have professional or social influence? The hairdresser, barista, or favorite clerk at the grocery store? How do we navigate those? And why do these people even make it into our circles if we aren't spending a lot of time with them? We do have to be mindful of how we spend our time, but it's important to remember that a relationship of any kind is never in vain. There is always the opportunity to extend God's love in both word and deed to the people we come in contact with. God places people in our path for a reason—and usually that reason involves some expression of love, service, or sharing our faith.

The relational tension we experience in our lives is typically due to uncertainty about how much time and energy we should routinely invest in these outer-circle relationships. There is no standard rule, but there are three questions to consider when you are trying to decide how to navigate between your inner-circle and outer-circle relationships in a way that honors both.

Questions as You Navigate Your Relationships

What is the state of your inner circle? This is affected by many factors, and no two inner circles look exactly the same. Some factors to consider include life stage, such as the age of your kids, whether or not you are still in college, where you are at in your career, and so on. The size of your family is another factor—someone with a larger family will obviously have more people in their inner circle, while someone with a smaller family may have more friends in their inner circle. You need clarity about your inner circle so that you do not overinvest in relationships of a lower priority. This is particularly important if your inner-circle relationships are suffering in any way. It makes no sense to spend more time with friends or at the office if your children need more of your time. Likewise, if your marriage is in a great place, then a getaway with the girls may be just what the doctor ordered.

Are you an introvert or an extrovert? How introverted or extroverted you are impacts the amount of relational energy you will have left over after you give what is needed to those closest to you. If you are an introvert with young children and work in a people-oriented job, then you probably won't have the energy for many more relationships at the end of the day. However, if you are an extrovert who thrives being around people, then your outer circle could easily be fuller because people energize you.

What is your relational capacity? Everyone has limits to their relational capacity. Some people have two or three close friends in their inner circle, while some people can handle eight to ten, or even more. There is no right or wrong number. Relational capacity is a reflection of life stage and personality. Being wise about your relational capacity means that you are able to connect the way you need to and in ways that best help others. If we're unwise, we might end up with several shallow relationships when what we really need is fewer but deeper friendships. The real trap is mistaking many outer-circle relationships for inner-circle friendships.

Navigating relationships in your inner and outer circles will often be challenging. Sometimes you might get the balance just right, and other times you might not. The main thing is to have grace for yourself. You are who you are, and the reality of where you are in life makes certain demands on you. And there will be times when shifting circumstances in your life — getting married, having kids, moving, getting a new job — will make you less available for some people. But don't let guilt add to the burden of transitioning between life's seasons. Relationships are a part of life, a part that is meant to be enjoyable and fulfilling. Relationships can also pose challenges and may take a lot of work, but always remember that the grace of God is enough for you and for others.

The quality and depth of your closest relationships will affect your pace in life because relationships are pacesetters. They can also be peace stealers—factors that sabotage rhythm and intentionality —when they are characterized by dysfunction. It's important to know the difference.

Relationship Peace Stealers

When the following characteristics define your closest relationships, they're peace stealers. This means they will be a continual source of strife and stress.

Sinful. If your closest relationships are bound together by activities that run against your conviction to follow Christ, they will eventually steal your peace and freedom. This is especially true if you are a new believer in Christ and God is calling you toward a way of living that is different from your old "normal." I'm not an advocate of leaving all your friends behind the moment you decide to follow Jesus. Part of our purpose in life is to be "salt that brings out the God-flavors in the world," and "light that brings out the God-colors" (Matthew 5:13–14 MSG). You have a sphere of influence that the greatest preachers and leaders on earth will never have access to, and God entrusts you with the privilege of making Him known in your world. But there does come a time when God calls us to travel life's roads to the beat of a different drum. The things that set the pace in our old life can't set the pace in our new life with Christ. When it's time to make a break, make it.

Even if you have been a believer for a while, you still need to assess the relationships that you currently have. Perhaps some of them might be keeping you from entering further into your relationship with Christ because they are against your convictions. Maybe you have friends who always gossip and criticize others, and when you are with them you just hope and pray they have something positive to say. It could be time to assess these relationships and decide whether or not they are causing you to enter into sin.

Crisis prone. There are some people who seem to be addicted to crisis—and I am not talking about folks who are going through a series of hardships. I am talking about people who are just not happy unless there is a storm cloud of drama following in their wake. If they happen to come into a calm environment, it won't be calm for long. They will make sure that everyone is stirred up about something by the time they leave. Crisis prone people are strife addicts, and they will bring that strife into your life as well.

Manipulative. Although there are people who have a legitimate right to be pacesetters in your inner circle, it doesn't mean they can use that place to manipulate you so they can get their way. People who do so are guilt-trippers, and they feel no remorse about co-opting your time, your resources, and your energy to achieve their goals. Don't let someone else set the pace of your life by manipulating you with guilt. By doing so, you will end up forfeiting the intentional shaping of your own life.

Disrespectful. A defining characteristic of fools in the book of Proverbs is that they show no respect for boundaries. They don't know when to be quiet, when to give up fighting, when to show respect, or how to act around their elders—they just don't seem to know or respect the boundaries of others or those required by the situation at hand. When people are used to trampling all over our personal boundaries, they can get angry when we start to reset or defend them. Whatever boundary they are used to trespassing over—be it time, personal space, or respect—is a resource they are helping themselves to at your expense and without your consent. When you reestablish and maintain your boundaries, you are basically taking that resource away from them—and no one likes to have things taken away. Expect some backlash and maybe a few explosions when you set boundaries. But stick with it— eventually, the boundary breakers will get the picture and look elsewhere to get their needs met.

If it is at all possible, keep relationships marked by these characteristics out of your inner circle. They can be part of your network of friendships, but that doesn't mean they warrant a daily or weekly investment. Because they tend to come with a certain amount of drama, we can spend too much time and energy on these relationships, which only diminishes our focus on the inner circle relationships that matter the most.

But what happens when the relationships that have a legitimate claim to be pacesetters in our inner circles are also peace stealers? What if the peace stealers who are in our inner circles aren't going anywhere? I don't have the answers to all of life's relationship questions, but I do know one thing. Jesus has all of the answers and is the answer. When our relationships aren't perfect (actually they are guaranteed not to be), His grace covers us. There are relationships that are always nonnegotiable, and they are not guaranteed to be healthy, but the Holy Spirit can and will navigate you well through life's relationship joys and challenges.

As we said at the start, relational wholeness is about having the right people in the right circle and investing in them at the right level. Sometimes what and who is "right" is difficult to know. The guidelines we've covered in the chapter so far can help us, particularly if we approach them prayerfully. Through prayer, ask God to guide you as you build up your family and inner circles. Whom do you spend most of your time investing in? Are you keeping your family and most important relationships first and leaving a legacy, or do you find yourself caught in a cycle of responding to the people who cry the loudest? Don't allow other people's crises and issues to shape the course of your life. Give that place only to the Lord and to those He has entrusted to your care.

Friendship is one important dimension of *shalom*. So is physical health. It's another pacesetter in our lives, and we'll look next at how being in a rhythm of good health practices can impact our lives in a positive way.

For Reflection

1. Using the relational concentric circles illustration as a reference, map out your relationships on a pad of paper. In what ways are you investing, or failing to invest, in the right people at the right level?

2. Who is in your inner circle? Do they have a legitimate claim to be pacesetters in your life?

3. What is your relational capacity right now? What factors are impacting your relational capacity?

4. What do you sense the Holy Spirit might be saying to you about your relationships?

Chapter 8

Your Body

*She girds herself with strength [spiritual, mental,
and physical fitness for her God-given task] and
makes her arms strong and firm.*

Proverbs 31:17 AMP

I struggled with the decision to include a chapter on health
because I knew I would have to be honest—honest about the fact
that this is an area of life in which I am still struggling. The best
way to describe my approach to health is consistently inconsistent.
I have consistently maintained inconsistent health habits since I
was twenty-seven years old. If you want to hear about people who
have conquered the mountain, there are a million others who are
more qualified than I am to lead the way.

Nevertheless, I just might be the best person to talk about it
because I'm guessing I am more the rule than the exception. I'm
like so many women in my season of life who used to be in shape,
but lost it all when we started having kids. I've struggled with
my weight my whole life. I love to eat and cook, and I hate to
exercise. I love to think about exercise. I love to get on Pinterest

and make Paleo diet and fitness boards. If you could be skinny by thinking about exercise and planning to do it, I would be a paragon of human fitness right now. But alas, one can only get fit by *actual* exercise and diet, and that's why I am not fit. (Except in my inconsistent times of consistent exercise.)

For the longest time, fitness wasn't a priority for me. Don't get me wrong. I wanted to be thin, but I didn't care if it came through crash dieting or exercising as long as it worked, and worked fast. The first time I really started to care about actually being fit was a few years ago on our third ski trip (back to skiing again!). We had just moved into a new house about six months before the trip. When we moved, I was in one of my "consistent" phases of health and exercising. I hung in there for a few months right after the move, but when we encountered some issues with the house that required extensive and unexpected renovations, I just gave up. I couldn't manage it all.

To top it off, I'm a stress eater. I've heard women who say things like, "I was so stressed out I forgot to eat—I just lost so much weight!" *Forgot* to eat? Forgot to get the carpets cleaned, sure. Forgot to change out of pajamas for the day—it's definitely been known to happen. Forgot to feed the dog, okay. But forgot to *eat*? How can a person forget that? Anyway, back to skiing. When we finally made it to the ski trip, I couldn't ski down the slope more than two times in a row without my legs turning into Jello. I was so winded just from carrying my skis to the lift that I had to take a short break before continuing along the flats to the lift line. And worst of all, nobody in my family wanted to be my ski buddy. "Mooooommmmm, you go too sllloooowwww!" So I spent most of the time in ski school or on the green slopes by myself.

My point is this: the condition of our bodies has a real impact on our ability to carry out the desires of our hearts. I love skiing, and I had been looking forward to it for months. I bought a brand-new ski jacket and new goggles. The weather was perfect. All the conditions were right for a great trip. But for all my desires and good intentions, I could not carry out what I purposed in my heart. My body just couldn't do it. My performance fell way beneath my skill level because I was so out of shape.

The connection between physical fitness and an ability to ski is obvious. Even though it may not be so obvious, our physical health also has an impact on the way we run our spiritual race. We are triune beings: body, soul, and spirit. But these parts of our being function interdependently with one another. We already know how the state of the soul can impact the body. For example, under stress, our shoulders tense up and pull forward. When we are at peace, we move at a more measured pace. When we are happy, we might experience a rush of energy and move at a faster pace. The impact our souls have on our bodies tends to be readily apparent, but what about the impact our bodies have on our souls?

It's not as easy to identify the ways our souls are affected by our bodies because the impact happens on the inside. But if you think about it, it's not difficult to see evidence of their interconnectedness. Maybe you can relate to some of these examples:

- When I am physically tired, I feel stressed and anxious because I'm afraid I won't be able to do all the things I need to do.

- When I gain weight, I feel insecure and less confident.

- When I am well-rested, I feel like I can conquer the world!

- When I eat well, I have more energy and feel better.

These are examples of what it means that, whether I like it or not, my body is a pacesetter for my life. Even though we can't control everything that happens to our bodies, we can do what is in our power to help them function in the healthiest way possible.

This means that we should work as best as we can to take care of them — they are spiritual structures!

God Values the Body

Christianity is wonderfully unique in the value it places on the physical body. Most people mistakenly believe that Christianity holds a dim view of the human body, even though two of its central beliefs — the incarnation and the resurrection — affirm the dignity and worth of our physical nature. Christian apologist Jill Carittini writes:

> What does it mean that Christ came in the flesh with sinew and marrow? What does it mean that he lived, breathed, and died and was raised *as a body*? Perhaps more importantly, what does it mean that the risen Christ *today*, as a corporeal being, is ascended and sitting at the right hand of the Father in heaven?[6]

We separate spiritual and physical, but they are not as separate as we suppose. The spiritual sanctifies the physical and makes it holy — a fact that is unique to Christianity.

The body is not the enemy of Christian spirituality. Our flesh doesn't corrupt our spirit, but in the saving of our spirits our bodies are redeemed and set apart as holy. The heavenly reality is not the body *absent*, but the body *incorruptible* (1 Corinthians 15:53).

While the state of my body has no bearing on my inherent worth or position in the kingdom of God, it has an undeniable impact on the way I experience and navigate the earthbound leg of my eternal journey. If we understand the purpose of our bodies and the high value God places on them, a desire to use them well should naturally follow. Perhaps one way to think about this is to ask: *When I value something, how do I treat it? How do I insist that others treat it?*

For example, I highly value the two white chairs in my living room. They have a cool, modern shape with braided leather trim. I love them because, for one thing, I designed them myself. In an otherwise traditional room, they add a little spunk and keep the space from being predictable and boring. I went back and forth over the decision to buy white chairs. With three small children in the house, I was almost certain they would soon be the victim of mud and melted chocolate stains. But I couldn't resist, so I gave in and bought them in spite of how impractical they were.

Here's how the chairs have survived for five years, through three toddler-hoods and numerous muddy shoes and spilled juice boxes: *value* and *protection*. I value those chairs, so I protect them from harm. I don't let the kids eat on them—ever. Period. I don't allow shoes on them—ever. Period. I don't allow markers, paints, or any other pigment-carrying creative utensils within a twenty-foot radius of them—ever. Period. For that reason, unlike my cheap family room sectional, which probably has the fungus version of Bigfoot living inside the cushions, these chairs have remained pristine, beautiful, and useful.

What we value, we protect. We cherish it, we nurture it, and we guard it from harm. If you don't understand the value God places on your body, it will be hard for you to make choices that protect it. Our choices about our health give witness to the heart-held belief that we are beloved and valued daughters of God and that every part of us matters to Him.

Have you ever thought about how you actually value your body? It is the one and only body you will ever have, and there is no price you can pay for a full replacement. Even when things are replaced (knees, hips, etc.), they never function like the original. When we are treating our bodies well on a consistent basis, we are pacing ourselves for wholeness in the long run. A healthy lifestyle that consists of a nourishing diet and regular exercise is a way to show God that we are thankful for the bodies He has given us.

In his first letter to the Corinthians, Paul describes our bodies as temples: "Do you not know that your bodies are temples of the Holy Spirit, who is in you, whom you have received from God? You are not your own; you were bought at a price. Therefore honor God with your bodies" (1 Corinthians 6:19–20). As temples of the Holy Spirit, we don't need to leave our ordinary, everyday lives and make a pilgrimage somewhere to experience God because God's Spirit resides within us. The Holy Spirit doesn't indwell us because we are holy; we are made holy by the fact that the Spirit indwells us. Living with the presence of God and carrying that presence to others so that it can have an impact on our world is the purpose of these bodies we live in. Like an actual temple, our bodies are holy spaces. We honor and worship God when we treat our bodies with care and respect.

Paul also likened our bodies to vessels that contain something precious: "We have this treasure in jars of clay to show that this all-surpassing power is from God and not from us" (2 Corinthians 4:7). There is nothing special about a clay jar; it's the most common of vessels, plain and unadorned. Our bodies are vehicles that have been commissioned to carry holy cargo. Of course, we don't confuse the value of the vessel with that of the treasure. But filled with a treasure of great worth, the vessel takes on the value of that which it carries. The fact that God has such a high view of the human body should encourage us to care for it by making a commitment to health as a pacesetter for our lives.

Four Pacesetter Practices for Physical Wholeness

Sleep, nutrition, exercise, and preventative care are four key factors in setting the pace for health and physical wholeness. The burnout, exhaustion, and spiritual slumps that rob us of *shalom* are often addressed if we simply pay adequate attention to these areas in our lives. If we handle them with intention and wisdom, we can minimize the potential that poor health or lack of physical fitness will sabotage our desires or the rhythms of grace in our lives.

Sleep

Sleep is one of the ultimate pacesetters in our lives. Scientists are not sure why we sleep, but they have developed several theories over the years. The one that makes most sense to me is called the Restorative Theory, which states that we sleep because we need to replenish and repair certain aspects of our bodies and our brains. Sleep contributes to healthy immune function and to restorative functions in our muscle growth and tissue repair, hormone regularity, and the synthesis of proteins into our bodies. When we are sleep-deprived, our ability to learn and perform tasks diminishes greatly.

It's believed that sleep is related to memory function as well, allowing us to consolidate and store new information and experiences so that they can be recalled at a later time. With all this knowledge about the benefits of sleep, you'd think it'd be a no-brainer that we'd make it a high priority. However, it's usually one of the first things we compromise, even though losing sleep probably undermines our wholeness more than any other factor.

The need to sleep is just another way that we are forced to come to terms with our limitations. Our limitations are what force us to choose which things we will focus on and which things we will let go of. We must choose because we can't do it all. The end of each day allows us to put our worries to bed with the sun and wake up to new mercies each morning. When we are well-rested, we are more patient and can enjoy our relationships more. Sleep sets the pace for whether or not we can move through the day alert and rested, or groggy and sluggish. Inadequate sleep can steal many things from our lives, especially our health.

Nutrition

A body properly fed is just as important as a body properly rested. To nourish means to sustain, strengthen, or build up. How often do we think about food doing this for our bodies? Do we eat with the intent to "sustain" our bodies? Or do we eat because we are hungry and want to temper the grumbling in our stomachs, or because it is fun and something that is socially celebrated? Furthermore, if we're already drained and exhausted, how often do we eat just to medicate our condition?

Practicing proper nutrition means that we are fully aware and engaged in the food choices we make. As our norm, we choose the apple over the packaged cookies and opt for the yogurt with berries over a dish of ice cream. We have all heard the phrase: *We should eat to live, not live to eat.* Food sustains our life, and proper nourishment sustains good health. Nutrition is a pacesetter because all food choices have a direct impact on our quality of life, good choices lead to lasting energy and longevity, and poor choices lead to fatigue and illness.

Exercise

Our bodies are meant to move, but most of us don't get enough physical exercise. We stand in lines, sit at desks, and wait in car lines and congested freeways. The answer, we know, is exercise.

If you have a set time to exercise every day but find yourself always canceling it or trying to fit in somewhere else, then this is not a pacesetter in your life. But if you have a set time to exercise and cancel or move things so that you don't miss your exercise time, then this is when it becomes a pacesetter for you. You have molded it into your schedule, and in turn it is now part of your rhythm. We truly are the only ones who can take care of our bodies; nobody else can do it for us. Picking up the dry cleaning, getting groceries, cleaning out the garage—these are part of life, yes, but someone else can do them or they can wait. Making health a priority means that we begin to see our bodies the way that God does—as vessels that are intricately crafted, incredibly valuable, and worthy of our time, attention, and loving care.

Shalom in this area of life means we have the energy and stamina to accomplish what God has in store. If we're not sleeping, eating, and exercising well, we'll struggle to keep the rhythm. The same is true with staying on top of our medical needs.

Preventative Medical Care

Once a year I have "doctor's week." I schedule all the appointments for proactive care such as teeth cleaning and mammograms. Do I like to spend this time and money going to these appointments? No, not really. But taking initiative to prevent illness is a way of living proactively. In the grand scheme of things, the amount of time and money spent is small in comparison to the cost—and consequences—of not doing preventative care. Will proactive medicine keep us from having illness or disease? No. But it will definitely help in some pretty significant ways.

There will always be aspects of our health that we cannot control. We may get sick or injured, for example. But what about the things we *can* control? Are we doing what we can with those things? And are we willing to start small? We have to move past the mental hurdle that we need a major overhaul or dramatic changes to make a dent in the health issues we struggle with. Believe it or not, small changes implemented consistently over time can have a big impact.

People exert tremendous effort and energy on using the latest fad diet to get fast results. The desire for fast results ultimately sabotages our efforts. If we would put the same effort and energy into establishing a rhythm of healthy living, the results would last longer and we would be healthier in the long run.

Health Peace Stealers

There was a brief moment in my life when I had mastered the discipline of healthy living. From twenty-one to twenty-five years of age, I was the healthiest I had ever been, or likely ever will be. I gained control of my exercise and nutrition habits during my last two years of college and held my ground until I got married. Actually, the decline started once Stovall and I started dating seriously. Before that, I went to the gym twice a day, morning and afternoon. Once we started dating, I knocked off the afternoon workouts and just did the morning ones. (Still pretty good!)

But over time, workouts got replaced with dinners out. Late nights edged out the early morning routines and I lost the habit of fitness altogether soon after our wedding day. By the time I had our first baby, nutrition and exercise were a thing of the past. I did not have room for them in my day—there was just too much going on. The test of something's value is the price we will pay to hold onto it. If we don't value our health, it will always get our leftovers, which means the pacesetter of health will be measured out by default rather than by intention.

Most of our default settings are not naturally inclined toward choices that lead to health. The apostle Paul acknowledged this when he wrote, "I discipline my body like an athlete, training it to do what it should. Otherwise, I fear that after preaching to others I myself might be disqualified" (1 Corinthians 9:27 NLT). Our bodies have to be trained to do what they should do. Not that we need a Bible verse to convince us of that. However, if we neglect them we will eventually become exhausted, burned out, and unhealthy. And aside from physical decline, our mental state will suffer as well because when we are making poor health choices, we can't help but think about how much we should try to get healthy. Or we beat ourselves up with guilt over the poor choices.

So the question is, Why don't we? There are a lot of possible answers that reflect different states of mind we might have. None of them will lead us to a place of *shalom*, so if you find yourself saying one or more of these, beware: you have a peace stealer on your hands.

I don't have time. For the most part, we know the general rules about healthy living. The problem isn't that we don't know what to do; it's that we don't do it. Most approaches to health work as long as we practice them consistently. The number one hurdle to establishing a rhythm of healthy habits is not knowledge, but time. We want the results, and we know what to do. But in order to say "yes" to health, we have to start saying "no" to some other things in our lives. Unfortunately, health typically loses in a battle of competing values.

Getting healthy can wait; I have other priorities right now. And it will ... until it won't. At some point the decisions we make in this arena of life will come to fruition. The seeds we sow—not the intentions we sow them with—are the deciding factor in the harvest we will reap. Health is not a competing value; it should be one of our main pacesetters. We should allow our health regimens to set the pace for how a good portion of the rest of our lives look.

I feel selfish making time for this. So many of us operate under the false assumption that caring for others requires denying ourselves. We feel selfish for prioritizing our health over almost anything else we are responsible for. But taking care of ourselves enables us to take better care of the people we love the most. It gives us the best chance of running our race for the longest amount of time and reaching our best potential. Think about flying in an airplane. The safety instructions pertaining to low oxygen or air pressure in the cabin always advise that we take care of ourselves first. That's because we cannot help others if we are passed out from lack of oxygen! Similarly, you cannot help or serve others at your best capacity if you are depleted and physically weak.

Pay Now or Pay Later

Our health is somewhat like credit cards. We can choose to pay now with the discipline and intentionality required to set a healthy pace, or we can choose to pay later with the consequences of continuing in patterns that lead to depletion and eventual burnout. When I was in college, I did what many college kids do; I signed up for my very first credit card. When I started using it, I couldn't believe how much fun it was to shop! I didn't have to look for clothes on clearance; I could actually buy what I wanted! It was a wonderful, liberating experience—until I got the first bill in the mail. You see, the spending was fun and the money actually wasn't real to me until I had to fork over the funds to pay the bill. In the same way, we "charge" things to our health. In our teen years and through our twenties we don't necessarily think of how exercise will benefit our bodies as we age, and we don't think of how poor nutrition will have lasting effects on our health. But in the end we will have to pay—and we can either pay routinely with proper nutrition and exercise, or we can pay later on in life by being overweight, out of shape, or sick.

Give yourself permission to make health a priority! When we are leading healthy lifestyles, we are healthy all around. Spiritual health and physical health can go hand in hand when we realize how much God values our bodies and we make valiant efforts to value them too. Valuing ourselves is part of the process of personal wholeness, which is what we will look at next. When we can evaluate and be honest with ourselves, we can make the changes that are necessary for living a healthy life.

If you are feeling anxious about establishing a rhythm of health in your life, you are not alone. It took me many years to establish a rhythm that worked for me. For a long time I went back and forth between seasons of extreme fitness and nutrition routines. It was an "all or nothing" mentality that I had. I did strenuous workouts for weeks at a time and then felt burned out and quit exercising all together. Then I would try on a pair of pants that were too tight, and out of my frustration I would commit to another round of extreme fitness routines. Do you see how the vicious cycle kept repeating itself? There's no *shalom* at the end of a yo-yo.

Finally, I realized that I needed to do what worked for me and stop trying to train for a triathlon every time I worked out. I started out on an elliptical machine for thirty minutes a day, four days a week for three weeks. I had to build myself up to be able to establish a rhythm that challenged me, but also allowed me to be in a place where I could consistently exercise at a sustainable pace. Eventually, I grew in my exercise capacity and I now regularly work out about one hour a day, four days a week. I have now learned to value exercise, not because I love it, but because of the way it makes me feel and the flexibility and strength it gives my body.

I also came to a point where I realized that I needed to give my body grace. I am not twenty-one years old anymore, and that is perfectly alright. What my body could do back then, it cannot do now, and I simply have to be content with that. The goal is to be at a place where I am doing what is right for my body, my age, and my season of life. I have to have realistic goals for myself because if I don't, I know I will never meet them. Realistic goals position me for the long run; they set the pace for a life of good health and longevity.

Good physical health is an attribute of being whole. When good health practices are a constant rhythm in our lives, we are freed up from the constant guilt of knowing that we are supposed to take care of ourselves physically, but not actually doing it. And more to the point, we will feel better and live stronger—enabling us to avoid the distractions of burnout and fatigue and really hold on to the adventure that God has planned for us.

In the next chapter we will look at spiritual vitality and the different parts of our lives that can together make us whole, healthy, and fulfilled. Without Christ, we are broken, cracked vessels; but when we allow Him to bring us to a place of personal wholeness, we are truly walking in rhythms of grace.

For Reflection

1. How would you describe your physical health right now?

2. What factors tend to sabotage your efforts to make health a priority?

3. What concerns you and what intrigues you about the idea of making healthy living a higher priority?

4. What do you sense the Holy Spirit might be saying to you about your health?

Chapter 9

Your Spiritual Vitality

They will be like a tree planted by the water
that sends out its roots by the stream.
It does not fear when heat comes;
its leaves are always green.
It has no worries in a year of drought
and never fails to bear fruit.

Jeremiah 17:8

I come from a long line of gardeners on both sides of my family, although you might not guess it by looking at my yard. I have the opposite of a green thumb; every plant I touch dies. My sister is the one who inherited all the gardening skills in our family. When I go to her house in the summer or over the holidays, I always enjoy going in her big backyard to see what she is growing. In the summer, she grows different varieties of tomatoes— huge heirloom species that weigh down the vines, and sweet little cherry tomatoes that grow on a bush and pop in your mouth with a burst of flavor. If you have never tasted a tomato straight off of the vine, take the next opportunity you get—they are delicious! My sister also grows cucumbers, summer squash, and green beans. All summer long the produce from her garden fills up baskets and bowls in her kitchen until they overflow. When they can't contain anymore, she gives the surplus to family and friends, who are always happy to relieve her of her extras. Fresh, homegrown produce is a gift.

Not everyone has the skill and patience to grow a fruitful garden. All those wonderful vegetables—tomatoes in the summer, eggplant and lettuce in the winter—don't just pop up out of the ground on their own. My sister has to create an environment that is conducive to growth. She has to test the soil to see how acidic it is and add things to it to balance out the pH levels if needed. She has to protect against pests in the summer and frost in the winter. She has to make sure that the plants get the right amount of water and sunshine. Come to think of it, I never did any of those things when I tried to grow a garden. I wanted to plant my seeds and forget about them until harvesttime, but that's not the way this whole gardening thing works. To have a garden full of life and fruitfulness, I would have had to create an environment conducive to growth. Let's just say, I am satisfied with the fruit and vegetables in the produce section of my local supermarket and the occasional trip to my sister's house where I can enjoy the fruits of *her* labor!

Unfortunately, we can't pick up spiritual fruit at the local supermarket. That would be convenient, but it's not the way this spiritual growth thing works. We have to grow it ourselves, in the garden of our own lives. And to do that, we have to create an environment that is conducive to spiritual growth by making spiritual disciplines a regular part of our life's rhythm. This is the way I want to live, and I bet this is the spiritual life you desire as well.

Cultivating an Environment
for Spiritual Growth

I can't imagine a better image of spiritual vitality than the one described in Psalm 92:

> But the godly will flourish like palm trees
> and grow strong like the cedars of Lebanon.
> For they are transplanted to the LORD's own house.
> They flourish in the courts of our God.
> Even in old age they will still produce fruit;
> they will remain vital and green. (Psalm 92:12–14 NLT)

Planted in the Lord's house, these godly people are flourishing, growing strong, producing fruit, and remaining vital and green their whole lives. These are not actions—things they are doing—but states of being and conditions of living. To be spiritually vital means that our condition is one of strength and continual growth. This kind of spiritual life overflows from unbroken fellowship with Christ as we keep pace with Him under the yoke of grace. It's not something we can force or control through spiritual practices. Rather, our spiritual practices, or spiritual disciplines, create an environment in which God can work—and spiritual growth and vitality are the outcome.

We want to experience a vibrant, satisfying relationship with God. Chances are that you chose this book because you want that kind of relationship with Him. Not once in twenty-five years of ministry have I heard a person say that his or her idea of spiritual fulfillment consists of compartmentalized, ritualistic habits. Yet this is exactly where practicing spiritual disciplines without paying attention to our spiritual vitality leaves us.

Have you ever felt stressed out by your relationship with God? If you have felt this way (or if you are feeling this way now), you might have invested too heavily in discipline without vitality. I did. Remember way back in chapter 1 where I talked about how the turning point in my journey came during a message my husband taught called "Project or Process"? I didn't realize it at the time, but I had unintentionally started to approach my relationship with God like a project that needed to be managed and completed. "Pray" and "work out" were right there next to each other on my to-do list. "Organize pantry" and "read Bible" were on the same line.

I had spiritual disciplines in place and I practiced them consistently, but I had put them on autopilot, checking off boxes on my reading plan, perfunctorily reciting names on my prayer list, and going my own way for the rest of the day. For the most part, I forgot about God until our next scheduled meeting. My relationship with God became something I did instead of my vital source for everything in life. It's definitely a good thing to have a structured approach to spiritual growth, but we set in motion a subtle drift in the wrong direction when we start to lump spiritual practices together with our other projects that need to be completed.

Projects and items on to-do lists are not rhythms; they are outcomes. What happens to completed projects? We cross them off our list and put them in the "done" category so we can forget about them. Think about it. Nobody cleans out the garage just so they can do it again the next day. You clean out the garage so you can forget about it and move on with the rest of your life—the fun, fulfilling, meaningful parts. The problem with putting your spiritual life on your project list is that your relationship with God starts to turn into one more thing you have to do before you can get on with the rest of your life.

Do you see where I'm going with this? Devotion without discipline won't produce growth. But what happens when we lose devotion and continue doggedly on with our routine without paying attention to our flagging spiritual vitality? God becomes just one more thing we do—a project we complete for the day and put away until the next time we have an appointment with Him.

So while we must consider spiritual disciplines as a pacesetter for life, let's keep the goal of those disciplines in mind. The goal of our spiritual disciplines is not the disciplines themselves, any more than the goal of my sister's garden is the soil, furrowed rows, and bean poles. The goal of our spiritual disciplines is spiritual vitality, just like the goal of the garden's structure is the life it contains.

Spiritual Disciplines for Growth

So what are spiritual disciplines? Whole books have been written on this topic! And I've included a list of several helpful resources in the appendix (pages 201–2). But let's take a brief look at eight disciplines as a starting point. Whether done individually or corporately, these are foundational practices for spiritual growth. Some, such as prayer and Bible engagement, are central to Christian practice. Others, such as fasting, might be optional for some but still enriching and significant for most of us to use at some point in our walk of faith.

Prayer. Prayer is talking with and listening to God. It can take many forms—thanksgiving, worship, praise, intercession (praying to God on another person's behalf), and supplication (praying for your own needs). It's important that we see prayer as the foundation for our relationship with God, and it is a key to experiencing *shalom.* Prayer not only covers our physical needs (Matthew 6:11; Philippians 4:6), but our spiritual needs as well, providing a way for the Holy Spirit to minister directly to our hearts (Romans 8:26).

Bible engagement. There are many ways to read and engage Scripture. For example, it can take the form of reading the Bible for general instruction and inspiration, usually according to a structured plan. Or it might involve a more focused Bible study in order to learn about a particular topic, doctrine, or person in the Bible. General Bible reading doesn't usually involve external sources, but Bible study often involves consulting sources such as Bible commentaries, Bible dictionaries, and other books by Christian teachers and scholars.

Meditation. Meditation is extended reflection and contemplation of Scripture. The Hebrew word the Bible uses suggests the image of chewing on something over again and again. Christian meditation is not to be confused with what we find in Eastern or New Age religions, which focuses on emptying one's mind and losing one's sense of self. Christian meditation is the opposite. As Christians, we are instructed to meditate on the Word of God and on God Himself (Joshua 1:8). Christian meditation is centered on intentionally filling the mind with a focus on some aspect of God or truth from Scripture, and then reflecting on it intentionally and deeply.

Self-examination and confession. In self-examination, we set ourselves before the loving gaze of God and invite him to search our hearts (Psalm 139:23–24). Even though the Holy Spirit is faithful to convict us of sin and guide us into truth, we are still exhorted to examine ourselves in God's presence so He can reveal any hidden faults, hurtful actions, or brokenness in our lives that requires repentance, healing, and restoration. Confessing our sins before God is part of this process and can be wonderfully liberating. We identify what's holding us back in our relationship with God while accepting the forgiveness He's already promised (1 John 1:9).

Fasting. Christians are encouraged to periodically abstain from certain foods or all foods for a set period of time. In a self-indulgent culture like ours, this might seem strange, but the idea is to clear the mind and heart and make space for prayer, spiritual breakthrough, and increased intimacy with God. Fasting can take many forms and is sometimes practiced in connection with self-examination. During Lent (the forty days preceding Easter each year), many churches invite congregants to engage in partial fasting as a corporate discipline. But individuals can fast whenever and however they feel the Holy Spirit leading.

Sacraments. A sacrament is an earthly sign associated with a promise from God. Virtually all Christian churches practice baptism and the Lord's Supper (also called communion or the Eucharist). Anglicans and the Roman Catholic Church also practice confirmation, penance (confession), anointing of the sick, holy orders (ordination of deacons, priests, and bishops), and marriage. Sacraments are part of the corporate expression of our faith as we participate in the local body of Christ. Communion in particular is intended to be taken regularly—one of the gifts of faith God gives to nourish our spirits.

Service. We serve each other by taking care of practical needs, praying for one another, and ministering to one another. We serve our communities by meeting the needs of the poor and oppressed and by sharing our resources with them and advocating on their behalf. We can also serve in the context of the local church with our spiritual gifts and callings to build and strengthen the body of believers to which we belong. Service is a means by which we intentionally follow in the footsteps of Jesus and give our lives for others.

Giving. Along with giving of ourselves in service, we are to give of our financial and material resources. We do this through tithes and offerings and by financially supporting specific works God has placed on our hearts. This is one of the means by which God builds His church and His kingdom. But it's also a means to form us spiritually. It's so easy for us to find our security in our bank accounts and investment plans. Giving helps to break the hold money has on us and lead us to rely on God as *the* source of our provision.

Individual and corporate spiritual disciplines like these work together to bring balance and wholeness to our lives. The individual disciplines keep us centered; the corporate disciplines keep us from being self-centered. The individual disciplines keep us rooted and grounded in faith; the corporate disciplines keep us rooted and grounded in love.

But how can you know where to start when it comes to making spiritual disciplines pacesetters for your life? That's what we'll consider next.

Going Green: Pace Yourself for Vitality

In order to experience spiritual vitality, we must set a life-giving and sustainable pace in our spiritual disciplines. In other words, our disciplines must be realistic. The performance pressure is off! (It was never really on you to begin with.) Spiritual disciplines are not projects for you to complete, but part of a lifelong process for you to engage in and enjoy. So take your time and go slowly. Choose one or two disciplines to start and establish a daily or weekly rhythm. Even annual rhythms—such as fasting for Lent —can be helpful.

As you consider which disciplines to start with, it's important to also consider your personality and preferences. For example, are you methodical, deliberate, and focused? Are you spontaneous and unstructured, and do you enjoy learning as you go? Do you like to wake up every morning knowing exactly what you are going to do for the day? Or do you like to have a general framework, but leave a margin for unexpected detours? As you choose your spiritual disciplines, give yourself permission to practice them in a way that honors your personality and your preferences. That doesn't mean you should never challenge yourself (fasting isn't typically anyone's preference!), but it does mean that you're more likely to sustain your practices if you engage them in a way that feels compatible with who you are as a person.

For example, prayer is a foundational spiritual discipline that all of us should work toward having as a daily rhythm. Prayer is easy and enjoyable for some people, like my husband. He loves to pray. He goes into his study and prays in a focused way for what seems like forever. But prayer is difficult for me—not because I don't like to pray, but because my mind is all over the place. I am a deep and fast thinker. After fifteen minutes I get bored, and by twenty minutes I'm usually off task entirely. I often joke that my ideas have ideas of their own. My prayers generate ideas as I pray them like popcorn kernels going off in my brain!

For years, I struggled with guilt and sadness because I couldn't sustain my focus in prayer. When I heard people talk about praying for an hour a day, I folded myself up in a bubble of silence until that part of the conversation passed. I didn't want people to know how difficult it was for me to pray. I was embarrassed by it. Then one day I was talking to one of my "praying" friends about some of the things I was learning in my daily Bible study. She said, "Wow, that seems like a lot. How long do you study?" "About an hour to an hour and a half a day," I replied. (I was in college then and had a lot more time on my hands!) Her response surprised me. "I wish I could study the Bible like that," she said. "It's such a challenge for me. I hate reading in general. Even reading the Bible is hard for me to focus on, but I love to pray!"

For the first time, I realized that not all people are meant to practice every spiritual discipline the same way. I gave myself the freedom and grace to approach prayer in a different way—a way that would help me anchor my wandering mind so I could focus.

I discovered that doing something physical while I prayed, such as pacing or walking around the block, redirected some of my excess mental energy and kept my mind focused on God. I learned that I could focus on prayer just as much as my "praying friends" if my body was moving. For a long time, I still felt as if I was cheating, but now I just accept it as part of who I am. God's grace is enough to close the gap and make up for what I am lacking. So that's what I mean when I say you need to engage spiritual disciplines in a way that is compatible with who you are as a person. Don't dilute them or dismiss them; just find a way to make them work for you.

As you consider the rhythm of your spiritual disciplines, you may find it helpful to work through the discernment questions that follow. I've adapted them from Marjorie Thompson's book *Soul Feast* and Adele Ahlberg Calhoun's book *Spiritual Disciplines Handbook*. As you make your choices, keep in mind that wholeness in this area is characterized by vitality and not only by discipline. Discipline serves vitality—not the other way around.

1. *How would you describe your current season of life?* Are you single and in school? Single and working? Married with kids? Married with *lots* of kids? Are you a single mother balancing the whole weight of parenting and providing? Or have you entered that happy state of grandparenthood (where things you would have disciplined your own children for doing have suddenly become adorable when your grandchildren do them)? Do you work full-time or part-time? Is your job nine-to-five behind a desk and neatly compartmentalized from the rest of your life, or is it 24/7 with life and work mixing up in a giant, happy mush?

2. *What natural strengths, gifts, and passions has God blessed you with?* Do you have a high degree of self-discipline? Easily identify with the pain and struggles of others? Love learning and studying? Feel drawn to prayer and meditation?

3. *Where do you sense God may be inviting you to stretch and*

grow? In what areas of life do you want to experience change? There is nothing wrong with choosing spiritual practices because they seem suited to your personality. However, they may not be the best practices to stretch you where you need it most. Consider, for example, the kinds of temptations you struggle with. Are you jealous of a particular person, or do you struggle to forgive people once they have hurt you? Understanding your weaknesses will help you determine where God wants you to grow.

4. *Are the disciplines you're considering realistic?* If you have a house full of preschoolers and toddlers, it may not be realistic to make an hour-long devotional part of your everyday routine. If you are pregnant or nursing, fasting is not a realistic option at this point. Especially at the beginning, the disciplines you choose should honor your situation in life and your personality. But eventually, spiritual practices must also address the areas in which you might be weak, or areas where you sense God is inviting you to grow or take on a new challenge.

5. *How will you practice the specific disciplines you have chosen?* For example, if prayer is your chosen discipline, will you journal your prayers, pray out loud, or pray silently? If you plan to engage the Bible, will your reading follow a structured plan, focus on a topic, or start with a specific book of the Bible?

As you work through these questions, the important thing is to stay focused on the primary point—to increase your spiritual vitality. It's not about your performance; it's about your potential. When I was a young believer, I spent so much time worrying about whether or not I was pleasing God that it robbed me of joy. I truly did not understand the fullness of God's grace. I put so much energy into trying to live up to this ideal of what I thought seeking God was supposed to be like that I rarely enjoyed His presence. Now I spend my energy on loving God and learning more about Him. The focus of my spiritual life is *Him*—not me!

Avoid the Peace Stealers

When it comes to spiritual vitality, there is no end of potential peace stealers. It's easy to forget that our spiritual life is one of warfare. The devil desires that we fail here more than in any other area. There is no point trying to catalogue every way he'd attempt to trip us up, but I'll offer just this. If any of these disciplines becomes a point of pride, accomplishment, or self-satisfaction, or if they start to become ends in and of themselves, then we've lost our *shalom*. There is no peace when we lose the point.

Practicing multiple spiritual disciplines at any given time is not the same thing as spiritual vitality. Remember, disciplines are tools that help us to put ourselves in a place where God can work, and they are structures designed to contain spiritual life. They are not items on a checklist of things we need to do to be spiritually healthy. They certainly are not a list of requirements to fulfill in order to be accepted and loved by God! They are like runways that give the grace of God a place to land in our lives so that we can experience it to the fullest.

Grace liberates. It does not oppress us or constrain us under heavy burdens. The yoke of Christ is the yoke of grace. It is the sufficiency of His work and His power for living in step with Him each day. Spiritual disciplines are the key for establishing, staying in tune with, and keeping in step with the divine tempo God sets for our lives.

—————— *For Reflection* ——————

1. What kind of environment have you created in your life for your spiritual vitality to work in?

2. As you read about the different spiritual disciplines, which ones appealed to you? If none of them appealed to you, can you think of a reason that might be so?

3. Work through the discernment questions for choosing a spiritual discipline (pages 137–38). What do your answers reveal about what you need right now in your relationship with God?

4. What do you sense the Holy Spirit might be saying to you about your spiritual vitality?

Part 3

SET YOUR RHYTHM — AND KEEP IT GOING

It's TIME TO GET DOWN TO THE NITTY-GRITTY OF CALENDAR management. Admittedly, this is where most people start. In fact, it's where I used to start. (Remember my caffeine-fueled sessions making life-management grids at Starbucks?) But calendar management does not set the pace for our lives. It's simply a structure created to hold the things we allow to set the pace for our lives. Now that we understand what our pacesetters are and how to manage them in a proactive way, we can begin building our calendars with a new goal in mind: *shalom.*

After getting an idea of what it takes to craft a new calendar, we'll consider additional ways to sustain the rhythms of grace in our lives. How do we know which opportunities to step into and which ones to pass by? How can we tell if we're losing our rhythm —and how do we get it back if we have? What is the one, key principle we can follow to hold on to wholeness? These are the topics we will explore together in this final section.

Chapter 10

Reboot Your Schedule

Teach us to number our days,
that we may gain a heart of wisdom.
Psalm 90:12

Perhaps you've played the video game called Tetris. Though my kids can't believe it, I used to play it when I was their age. It was the default game on the Nintendo Game Boy, which was invented shortly after dinosaurs walked the earth. If you've played it, you know that the goal of the game is to arrange free-falling game pieces (called Tetriminoes) into a horizontal wall with no gaps. The Tetriminoes are composed of four connected blocks arranged in various shapes. They fall at random, and as they do the player must try to find the perfect fit for each piece. If each piece is successfully placed into the right space, the outcome is a perfectly horizontal line.

Does this process sound familiar? It should, because it's how most people—myself included—approach managing their schedules. We look at all the opportunities and obligations coming at us and try to make them fit into the empty spaces on our calendars. Ah, but the similarities don't end there.

Once the player builds a perfect horizontal wall with no gaps, the wall disappears and the player must begin to build the wall again. The same thing is true for every perfectly scheduled and productively maximized week we achieve—it simply disappears into the next week ... and the next ... and the next ... and the next. If we haven't used our time to build something intentionally with lasting value, then all we get for our efforts is one more week of a clean slate to fill up again.

No one ever wins at Tetris. The longer you play and the higher you go, the faster the pieces start to fall. It gets increasingly difficult to fit the odd shapes together. Theoretically, if players could continue to align all the falling pieces without fail, they could play on into infinity. And what would they get in return? Just more pieces, falling faster and faster in increasingly odd shapes and complex patterns.

This is exactly the way our schedules work. The better we get at managing our work flow and our time, the more opportunities come our way. This is a good thing, but it also makes life more complex. In the end, everything centers around playing the game —just trying to make sure all the pieces fit and none fall through the cracks. But they will fall through the cracks. The escalating challenges soon become impossible to overcome. Schedules fill up, gaps form, and things begin to collapse.

Between Time and Space

Time management is big business because people are desperate to conquer time, and "conquering" is actually something we humans are made to do. When God placed Adam and Eve in the garden of Eden, He gave them a mission: take dominion and subdue (Genesis 1:28). Another word we could use to describe this mission is "conquer." However, it's important to note that what God told humans to conquer was space—the land, the animals, and the earth with all it contains. We still do this today. Think of all the ways we conquer the material world—everything we can see, feel, and touch—by trying to manage it.

But for all of our God-ordained conquering of space, we were never meant to conquer time. "We cannot conquer time through space," through either pyramids or fame, says Abraham Joshua Heschel, a Hasidic Jewish rabbi in his book *The Sabbath*. "We can only conquer time through time."[7] We can't manage time in the same way we manage space. It can't be squeezed into spaces that are too small and be negotiated into giving us a better rate of return on our investment. It can't be multiplied. It can't be stored for later use. We can't stop it or start it. We can't speed it up or slow it down. Not one of us will ever truly own one hour, one minute, or one second of time exclusively for ourselves.

God gave human beings dominion over the earth (space), but He alone has dominion over time. In our race to subdue the earth, to multiply and increase our space, we trade on credit the only thing we can't multiply—time. God gave the world of space to Adam and Eve, but He kept time for Himself. Time belongs to God alone; that is why we will never be able to conquer it.

If we can't manage time, if we cannot conquer it, then what can we do with it? We can only solve the problem of time through "the sanctification of time,"[8] says Heschel, which sounds close to what the Bible says: "Redeem the time" (Ephesians 5:16 NKJV). To sanctify or redeem time means to set it apart for holy use.

Heschel describes Judaism as a religion that teaches its followers to be attached to holiness in time instead of holiness in space. Starting with the weekly rhythm of Sabbath, God identifies times that are to be set apart—or sanctified—to worship Him. These times are not given to God because they are holy. They are holy because they are given by God and set apart—or sanctified—to

God. Rabbi Heschel calls the days of the Jewish calendar "our great cathedrals" and compares them to sanctuaries.[9]

Isn't that a beautiful image of what time can be? A sanctuary is a place of divine habitation, the holiest place within a temple. The word "sanctuary" also carries the meaning of protection and refuge. But for most of us, time is the furthest thing in the world from a divine refuge. Instead, it's a scarce commodity shot through with loud alarms, impending deadlines, and the ticking hands of the clock. Perhaps this is why we want so desperately to conquer it. Yet, the same minutes that press us forward to the next task or meeting, even as they slip through our grasp, have the potential to be sanctuaries—places of respite and communion —if we set them apart for God and make them available as a place for *shalom* to take up residence.

I used to think of my relationship with God as one thing and my schedule as another thing. Outside of spending time with God each day and going to church on a regular basis, the two seemed disconnected. At most, a routine weekly schedule provided a framework for scheduling activities related to my spiritual life. There was a perfect space for daily spiritual disciplines like prayer and Bible reading. Small groups squeezed into a neat little spot on Wednesday mornings. Sunday, of course, was a big block of church time. Still, even these times assigned to things labeled "spiritual" often stressed me out because I didn't see them as productive. There were always so many "real" things to get done, things that mattered—in other words, things that would show up in my world, the realm I rule, which is the world of space. That's kind of sad, when you think about it, isn't it?

Everything began to change for me when my eyes were opened to a new way of seeing the relationship of time and spirituality. The apostle Paul urges us to "fix our eyes not on what is seen, but on what is unseen." His reason? "What is seen is temporary, but what is unseen is eternal" (2 Corinthians 4:18). I came to realize that the way I view time and my relationship to it is not merely a framework for managing my "spiritual" activities; it is actually a profound reflection of my spiritual life.

To see things that are unseen is a tall order. How are we supposed to do that? We have to use a different lens for viewing the world around us. We must learn to see it and value it from the vantage point of eternity. We grow in our ability to see the unseen things of eternity as we align our vision of this temporal world with the Father's vision of it. What is His vision of this world? It is His glorious, beautiful, broken, fragile, precious creation ... and it's temporary. It is fading away. So we should love it. Enjoy it. We should fully delight in God's amazing world and in every single second of time we have been given to inhabit it. But remember —always—this isn't all there is. To be truly free is to live with a conviction of this truth.

As we turn now to the process of crafting a schedule, I invite you to think of the empty spaces between the lines on your calendar in a different way than perhaps you have thought about them in the past. Instead of seeing them as empty rooms waiting to be filled, try seeing them as something more concrete. Try seeing each day as the wood and stone with which you are building the temple of your life on earth. What kind of temple do you want to build? Just like the Sabbaths are temples in time for the Jewish people, your schedule is a framework for the temple you are building with your life. It's a temple made not with bricks and mortar, but with minutes, hours, days, and years.

The Seven-Step Reboot Process

The process of building a *Rhythms of Grace* schedule requires time as well as substantial prayer, thought, and planning—and then usually more prayer! Rather than diving into the nuts and bolts now, I want to walk you through an overview of the seven-step process to give you an idea of what the reboot is and why it's important. Then, when you are ready to reboot, there is a spiffy Reboot Guide in the appendix that will guide you through the whole process step-by-step.

STEP 1: Identify Your Theme for the Year[10]

Identifying a theme serves as a compass for planning your year. Begin by reviewing your responses to the questions at the end of each chapter. Pay attention to any common issues, words, or phrases that show up in your answers. For example, if the words "balance" and "rest" appear over and over again, it could be that God is inviting you to pay attention to these issues in the year ahead. If so, your theme compass would point you to prioritizing changes that will lead you toward balance and rest.

STEP 2: Get the Big-Picture Perspective

Now step back and consider the big picture of your year as a whole. The goal overall is to establish *patterns* that lead to wholeness. To do that, you first need to see the big-picture perspective of where you are right now and where you want to be in the year ahead.

Use the questions in the Reboot Guide to help you reflect on the larger context of your life. They are designed to help you be realistic about what you can accomplish over the course of the next twelve months so that your goals are achievable. They can be challenging, especially if it's been a long time since you've had a chance to be still and think about things deeply. If you feel stuck on a question, simply move on to the next one; you can circle back later to any questions you skip. The main thing is to allow sufficient time to work through the questioning process and to have patience with yourself throughout the process.

STEP 3: Identify and Prioritize Your Pacesetters

Identify the pacesetters you need to prioritize and the action steps that will help you move toward wholeness (*shalom*) in each area of your life. First you will spend some time defining what wholeness in each of your pacesetters would look like. Then you will establish goals and action steps to help meet those goals. Finally, you'll work through a card-sorting exercise that will help you choose your top one or two pacesetters.

STEP 4: Establish an Annual Rhythm

Having clarity about your pacesetters and about the big picture provides an essential framework to help you put your monthly, weekly, and daily rhythms in context. It allows you to see the blueprint of what you are building before you choose the wall art. I have found that most people tend to want to go straight to filling in each day in chronological order month by month, but our more frequent rhythms are equivalent to the wall art, not the blueprint. That's why we work on the annual schedule first.

Take a look at your next twelve months and write down in your calendar all the nonnegotiable events and other dates. This includes birthdays, holidays, anniversaries, important school dates for your children, as well as any extracurricular activities. Include dates and events connected only to your inner circle and closest friends. Sometimes we assign the label "have to" to things that fill up the calendar just because that's the way we've always done it. If your calendar looks overwhelming and overbooked at this first stage, it might be time to reconsider some of your nonnegotiables.

STEP 5: Set Your Pacesetters

Once you have an idea of what your annual rhythm looks like, it's time to find the best way to place your pacesetters into your schedule. The Reboot Guide includes assessment questions to help you evaluate your pacesetters and place them in the right space.

STEP 6: Establish Your Weekly Rhythm

To construct a weekly rhythm, you'll take stock of what things need to happen each week and then prioritize those things on your calendar. It's important to focus on weekly rhythms before monthly or daily rhythms for three reasons:

- Daily rhythms are what make up our weekly rhythms. So when we establish weekly rhythms, we are actually also capturing daily patterns in the same step.

- Not everyone has monthly rhythms, or your monthly rhythms may not be the nonnegotiable ones. For example, you have a standing dinner date with friends every month. That's a great relational monthly rhythm. But if you had to make a trade-off one week, say, for your child's dance recital, it would probably be easy to see that the dance recital should take top priority.

- Our ability to commit to important monthly rhythms often depends on what our weekly rhythms look like. Of course, some people have important monthly rhythms. Perhaps, for example, you share the care of elderly parents with your siblings, and once a month you take your parents to doctor appointments or on errands. However, before you could even choose the best day to agree to commit to this monthly rhythm, you would need to know, in general, what your weeks look like. So starting with weeks is the most logical place to begin.

There are some vital pieces that should set the foundational rhythm of a weekly schedule. They include:

- *A Sabbath zone:* Every week should have a Sabbath zone, which is a dedicated period of rest and renewal.

- *Priority pacesetters:* If your priority pacesetters (the top two pacesetters you identified in step 3) are not already a part of your weekly rhythm, they should be.

- *Flex zones and weekend zones:* These zones are planned margins. You can't plan for the particulars but you know something will pop up. Flex zones are places where you schedule margins that you know you'll need before you need them. Weekend zones are a kind of catchall space for celebrations, kids' activities, and catching up on tasks and projects.

- *Look-ahead zone:* This is dedicated time to look ahead into the next week. Ideally, this should occur at the end of your work week.

STEP 7: Establish Your Daily Rhythms

So now it's time to schedule your days. You start with your pacesetters and then the big things you need to do each day. You will probably discover that certain parts of the week are faster moving and other parts slower.

So that's the basic overview of the schedule reboot! The reason we all need a reboot is because life has a way of getting crazy and we have a crazy way of reacting to the craziness. Craziness throws us into a reactive *pattern* and causes us to lose focus on the things that really matter. It happens to me. All. The. Time. So to keep my focus, I make these reboots a biannual rhythm. Twice a year,

I sit down with my calendar and my pacesetters and go through this exact process.

You don't have to do more than one reboot a year, but most likely you would benefit from two. Waiting a full year has the potential of taking you back to square one each time. In fact, many people I've worked with say that they begin to feel the full impact of the reboots at the third one. That's when the accumulated momentum of all this intentional thinking and planning starts to show results. But you do have to be patient and commit to engaging the process over the long haul to experience those results.

When I first started working through this process, I actually did reboots three or four times a year. My children were younger then, and change was more frequent. I had a lot less control over my schedule, so I needed to make adjustments more frequently. To be honest, thinking about my life in this way was a skill I was almost forced to grow into. Some of the things I thought would happen in my life didn't. Sometimes I got overly ambitious and tried to tackle too many goals. Other times, I wasn't fully in touch with what I really wanted, and it took a couple of reboots to gain clarity on the life I ultimately envisioned.

The practice of routine reboots has helped me to establish a rhythm of prayerful self-reflection and self-awareness. Reboots give me a practical way of making sure that what I am doing is aligned with what God wants for me and what I want as well. The end result is that I have greater confidence in my boundaries and in the choices I make because I understand the "why" behind those things.

EIGHT KEY TIPS FOR SCHEDULING

No matter how your rhythms shape up, here are eight key tips that will help you to maintain a life-giving schedule.

1. *Take notes as you go.* As you begin this journey of establishing new rhythms in your schedule, it's important to document what works and what doesn't work. You don't have to make changes immediately if you don't want to, but if you notice something isn't working for you, write it down so you can remember to change it later on. If something works well, write that down too and note what you like about it so you can put it into practice in other areas.

2. *Don't give your best energy to things that are predictable and repeatable.* There are certain things that you know without a doubt are going to happen on a predictable and repetitive basic. My go-to example is dinner. Dinner is predictable; it is always going to happen without fail. We know this to be true. It's also repetitive: it happens every day; this we also know. And yet how many nights do you find yourself standing in front of an open refrigerator or pantry wondering, *What in the world are we going to have for dinner tonight?*

Everything that is predictable and repeatable can be planned and systematized. It doesn't have to take up one additional ounce of your mental or emotional energy if you don't want it to. I used dinner as an example, but there are plenty of other predictable, repetitive things that are less mundane. Birthdays and anniversaries? They happen every year, same date, same people. Christmas and other holidays? Every year, same date, same people. All of these things are predictable and repetitive. So unless you just love feeling caught off-guard at the last minute, put them in a system, plan ahead, and free up all that energy for other things that matter more to you. Give your best energy to things that move your life forward.

3. *Limit what you say yes to.* Everything you say yes to requires saying no to something else, such as rest or time with your inner circle. Make sure you're saying no to things that don't support your goals or ongoing rhythms so you can spend your limited time and energy on what's most important to you.

4. *Leave yourself some margin.* A margin is simply a little empty space that gives you room to be flexible. Don't feel compelled to fill every blank space on your schedule. You need blanks. A margin is good and healthy. Don't race to fill it. Also, when you set aside time for something in your weekly schedule and it gets moved or canceled, leave that space open —don't fill it up with other things. For example, if you have a monthly lunch planned with a friend and she can't make it next time, don't jump to fill the slot with something else. Consider it a gift of margin and don't spend it too quickly.

5. *Establish a weekly attendance limit.* Decide ahead of time what your upper limit is for the number of events and activities you will attend each week. How many birthday parties and baby showers will you attend? How many nights a week are you willing to be away from home? If you set your upper limit, this will give you a reference point when you are trying to weigh your options.

6. *Make nightly resets part of your daily routine.* A good day starts the night before. Take the pressure off your morning rush by doing everything that has to be done before you leave the house the night before. Pack the lunches. Pick out your clothes. Organize the briefcase. It makes a huge difference to wake up every morning prepared for the day instead of scrambling around to finish everything you need to do before flying out the door.

7. *Look for bookends.* When making a commitment on your schedule, first take a step back and look at what bookends the empty space you are about to fill. For example, maybe a friend invites you to attend an event with her on a Monday night. Technically, you might be free. But on Sunday you have church and lunch with another friend afterwards, and you know that you will need to go visit your grandmother in the hospital after her surgery, which could end up being a late night. Monday is a regular day at work, but Tuesday you are expected to present a proposal to your supervisor. Yes, Monday is free, but it is bookended by some pretty busy days. Try to imagine how you will feel Monday night during the event you are being invited to. Maybe you are full of energy and being out and about will energize you even more. But maybe you will end up wishing you were curled up in bed in your pajamas watching *Seinfeld* reruns with a cup of hot tea. I know which end of the spectrum I would fall on (bonus points if you guessed the pajamas option!), but everyone is different. Know your weekly limits as well as your daily limits and allow yourself some breathing room between the busyness.

8. *Get off the performance grid.* This process is *not* meant to serve as a way to make you feel ashamed or stressed about all the things you haven't done or that you still need to do. I can't state that strongly or often enough. You will reflect on changes you need or want to make and some of the ways that your current situation differs from the reality you want. In that process, it's easy to get discouraged or feel overwhelmed. It might seem simpler to avoid the process altogether and go back to the way things were before. Believe me, I understand! But your schedule is not a performance grid. Nor is it a yardstick to measure how good or bad a person, wife, mom, employee, or leader you are. This whole process is a way for you to become proactive in building the life you want under the guidance and direction of the Holy Spirit and with the box top of *shalom* in clear view.

Four Habits of Perspective

I conclude each reboot by engaging in four habits of perspective. It's a process that brings clarity and focus to everything the reboot process revealed to me. As I reflect on these questions, I write down all my answers in a journal so I can reflect on them at the next reboot. From reboot to reboot, then, is a big circle of growth that feeds into itself and builds on its own momentum. Here are my four habits of perspective.

HABIT 1: Celebrate Good Things, Grieve Losses, and Release the Past

Each season of life has its ups and downs, its high points and low points. Taking time to reflect on these things every few months serves two purposes. (1) It gives me a space to celebrate the good things that have happened in my life. I want these good things to become part of my memories. I don't want to forget the beautiful little moments of God's goodness woven throughout my days. (2) It gives me the chance to grieve disappointments and lay them to rest. There are times when struggling to fix something, or forcing a relationship, or figuring out why it had to happen that way must come to an end. There is a time to say, *It is enough. I commit this to your hands, Father. Selah.* When I practice this habit of perspective, I accept the past for what it is and let it go so I can enjoy the present more fully.

HABIT 2: Receive and Renew My Vision for the Future

I actively dream about what I want my future to be like in specific terms. What memories do I want to create with my children before they leave the house? What travel destinations belong on my bucket list? Where do I want to be at the next stage of my career? At the end of my career? I also consider questions like these: What do I want to feel like at the end of this year? What do I hope to accomplish? What do I hope is no longer part of my life? In three to five years, what major milestones will happen in our lives?

These are long-range considerations, but remember that you are not making goals or action steps here. You are just making it a habit to think about your preferred future in specific terms. This is called "dreaming." Sadly, we often lose the skill for doing it well as we grow up. Practicing this habit of perspective just might help you get it back.

HABIT 3: Realign My Present Realities with the Future I Envision

After looking back at the past (habit 1), and then forward to the future (habit 2), I turn my attention to the present. As I look to the present in light of the past and future, I can thoughtfully consider questions like these:

- Am I focusing on the right things now to create the future I am envisioning, or am I just reacting to what comes my way, catching the balls being thrown at me?
- Does my calendar reflect my priorities and my purpose, or just my obligations?
- What can I learn from the last few months to make the present better?

HABIT 4: Refocus on *Shalom*

Even though I have just finished some really intense calendar planning, I want to be sensitive to the Holy Spirit and leave room for any adjustments He leads me to make, so I spend time in prayer, asking the Lord to order my steps and submitting the plans of my heart to Him. When I focus on *shalom*, I make sure that the things I am doing (and planning to do) are in fact leading me *toward* wholeness and not away from it.

This perspective is essential for keeping the right box top in front of me as I build my life. Now when I look at all the pieces of my life spread out across the table, I don't get as overwhelmed by them as I did when I was an eleven-year-old girl sitting at my grandmother's kitchen table. I know there is a bigger picture. I know that the big picture is *shalom*. Peace and wholeness. Nothing lacking; nothing lost. And I can say with confidence, *This might look messy right now, but it's going to be beautiful when it's done.*

We cannot conquer time. We can only sanctify and redeem it. Our time on this earth is as fleeting as a vapor, yet our lives are eternal; they will continue on the other side of the veil. Let's not allow a schedule to overshadow the truth that the pace of our lives can be sacred. I'm sure you realize after going through this chapter that it's easier said than done. Don't get hung up on that. The reality is that it *can* be done — more and more women I know are doing it all the time. And it works! So be encouraged. God controls time, but He has given us ways of making it count for us and for our peace.

For Reflection

1. How do you respond to the idea that you cannot conquer time—that time belongs to God?

2. In what area of your life do you most need to experience what Rabbi Heschel describes as a sanctuary in time?

3. How do you feel about the idea of a schedule reboot? What appeals to you about it? What concerns might you have?

4. What do you sense the Holy Spirit might be saying to you about your schedule?

Chapter 11

Consider
Your Opportunities

People do their best making plans for their lives,
but the Eternal guides each step.

Proverbs 16:9 The Voice

I remember the day we finally found *the house*. It was 6:00 in the
evening, and the sun was just beginning to set. We had been looking at houses all day in the same neighborhood and found nothing
we loved. I was discouraged, tired, and ready to call it a day. I
almost skipped this last showing on the list, but at the urging of
my husband and the real estate agent, I agreed to do a quick walk
through of one more house.

The minute I opened the door I knew this was it. I could just
feel it. Have you ever had a moment like that? It wasn't one particular thing that sold me on the place. The colors were garish,
the layout had some issues, there were ... smells. There was just
something about the whole package that drew me in. The way the
setting sun cast a glow over the living room, the wide hallways

perfect for running kids, the giant oak tree dripping with Spanish moss in the backyard ... all of these things came together in a way that spoke to my soul. *Welcome home.* I could imagine the foyer littered with backpacks and shoes and birthday parties in the backyard. *Life can happen here.*

I was so excited about finding a house I loved that I missed one important detail: the doors on the hallway bathroom. The hall bath is a quirky little feature of our home. It is a small, pass-through bathroom with a door on each side that can be entered from the family room or the central hall. It's not private at all, and it's the only bathroom in the house that can be accessed without going through a bedroom. So I don't know how I missed the fact that both doors on the bathroom were *glass doors*. Yes, you read that correctly. The bathroom doors were inset with a large solid panel of glass. It was frosted glass, but believe me, it wasn't frosted enough to ensure total privacy. When the lights were on, you could see what was going on in there. Needless to say, we replaced the glass doors with wood doors once we moved in.

I share this story because it reminds me of how I tend to respond to the opportunities that come my way. When I am excited about a new opportunity, I often miss important details that later come back and (unpleasantly) surprise me. Opportunities can be open doors into a new season, or they can be revolving doors that swing us right back around to the place we just left. Either way, they almost always bring challenges that require more time and attention than we anticipated.

For example, I might be invited to speak at an exciting new conference and say yes without realizing that the dates fall right between a major project deadline and a big event at church. Suddenly, my new opportunity looks a lot more like a big hairy burden. Or what if you were offered a job promotion with higher pay and benefits, but you knew it would require working longer hours and spending less time with your family? If you really thought about it, you might conclude that the promotion doesn't look as attractive anymore. Whatever the opportunity—moving to a new location, building a new relationship, starting a new initiative —there will be costs as well as benefits.

None of us wants to remain static in life, and it's good to step out in faith and stretch ourselves with new challenges, but we also have to be wise about our choices. So how do we know which opportunities to step into and which ones to let go of? And how do we maintain healthy rhythms of grace through it all?

Good Opportunities or God Opportunities?

An opportunity, by dictionary definition, is an appropriate or favorable time or occasion, a situation or condition favorable for the attainment of a goal, good position, or prospect. During His time on earth, Jesus had many opportunities and accomplished a great deal. In fact, the gospel of John says that if all the works Jesus did were written down, there wouldn't be enough books in the world to contain them (John 21:25). But even with all the things Jesus did beyond what is recorded in Scripture, there were still lots of things He *didn't* do. Consider the sick He did not heal, the people He did not stop to have conversations with, or the dead He did not raise to life. Jesus passed through throngs of people all the time, and not all of them received healing. He healed one lame man at the pool of Bethsaida, but the Bible tells us that there were many sick, lame, and blind gathered there. I don't know why Jesus chose that one man over all the other people at the pool, but I do know that Jesus was never in the habit of doing things just because He could.

Take, for example, what happened at Capernaum, a town in

Galilee. People believed in Him and many were healed. Everything was going great, and there was a lot more work Jesus could do to help the people there. The Galileans were a perfect fit for His mission: the poor, the captive, and the brokenhearted. They urged Jesus to stay with them longer, but instead He chose to leave, saying to His disciples, "Let us go into the next towns, that I may preach there also, because for this *purpose* I have come forth" (Mark 1:38 NKJV, emphasis added).

Or how about the time His brothers tried to convince Him that a trip to Jerusalem during the Feast of Tabernacles would be the perfect opportunity to take His ministry public? He declined, saying, "Now is not the *right time* for me to go" (John 7:6 NLT, emphasis added).

Even when Jesus heard that Lazarus was deathly ill, He delayed his visit by two days. Jesus said, "This illness does not lead to death. It is for the glory of God, so that the Son of God may be glorified through it" (John 11:4 ESV). Jesus loved Lazarus and his sisters, Martha and Mary. Yet He delayed coming to heal Lazarus and even allowed him to die. Why? Because there was a greater purpose to be fulfilled. "Then Jesus told his disciples plainly, 'Lazarus has died, and for your sake I am glad that I was not there, so that you may believe'" (John 11:14–15 ESV).

To most of us, all of these events would have appeared to be good opportunities, open doors full of potential that could move Jesus' ministry forward. But He walked away from them. How did Jesus know which opportunities to take and which ones to pass by? How was He able to discern what was and was not the right timing?

He did it by listening to and depending on God. Jesus remained in unbroken fellowship with His Father, listening for guidance and remaining fully dependent on Him. He said, "I tell you the truth, the Son can do nothing by himself. He does only what he sees the Father doing" (John 5:19 NLT). And, "My nourishment comes from doing the will of God, who sent me, and from finishing his work" (John 4:34 NLT). Do you see how Jesus modeled carrying the yoke of grace? He only did what He saw His Father doing—nothing more. This is how He evaluated the opportunities presented to Him, weighing whether each one was a *good* opportunity or a *God* opportunity. Though the opportunities presented to Jesus were valid and good, by keeping in tune with His Father, He knew that some were not essential to His purpose.

We must know what we are called to do and who we are called to be, or we will rush heedless through every open door that presents itself, only to end up exhausted and frustrated at our lack of impact. We must also be mindful of our season of life; some opportunities might be good now, but best seized at a later date according to God's timing. During seasons of waiting for the right timing God prepares and positions us to steward the opportunities He brings our way.

The Three Components
of Fruitful Opportunities

There are times in our lives when opportunities are scarce and we jump at the first thing that rolls along. Then there are other times when we have more opportunities than time or resources. In either instance, we need help choosing the right opportunities. In my experience, the most fruitful opportunities to invest in occur where *purpose*, *preparation*, and *positioning* meet. Let's take a close look at these three factors.

Purpose

Your purpose is God's unique call on your life. It is the means by which God enables you to invest in the lives of others. Purpose emerges from your unbroken fellowship with Christ, and it involves much more than simply identifying what you're good at or what your gifts and talents might be. Your purpose is what you were put on earth to do, but it's important to clarify that your purpose is not your job description. Job roles will continually shift, depending on the season for you, your family, or your employer. Your job is a vehicle or means by which you might accomplish your purpose, but your purpose will always point toward something greater. By staying in unbroken fellowship with Jesus, you can continually make room for your purpose to shift and grow.

During the early years when my husband, Stovall, and I were planting Celebration Church in Jacksonville, Florida, I had a young toddler and spent the bulk of my time as a full-time, stay-at-home mom. I wanted to do more for the church and spend more time "in the trenches" with the other staff and volunteers, but I simply couldn't afford the energy or time. Yet, God still had a purpose for me during that season at home. My purpose was not only to care for my child, but to allow God to do something *within* me. He was developing my heart and my character, preparing me for the next opportunity.

If I had chased a ministry endeavor in that season, it would have been birthed out of my flesh and not sustained in the long run. Jesus tells us, "Flesh gives birth to flesh, but the Spirit gives birth to spirit" (John 3:6). When you begin a ministry in your flesh—your own strength, drive, agenda—you will have to sustain it in the flesh. What is birthed from the Holy Spirit—directed by God's power, peace, purpose—will be sustained by the Holy Spirit. The demands of regular life are actually already more than we can handle on our own; when you're following Jesus, new opportunities need to be Spirit-born and anchored to God's purpose for that time.

Fast forward several years to the present, where God has given me the opportunity to work in ministry full-time. I've been entrusted with leadership oversight for key ministry areas of the church, have two more kids, and am in a position to launch new ministry initiatives. Within my sphere of influence, I have the privilege of being a pastor to the girls and women at our church. I also have incredible opportunities to speak into the lives of women around the world. I absolutely love seeing the daughters of God realize and live out the fullest potential of who they are in Christ. Any gift, talent, or skill God has entrusted me with serves to accomplish this purpose. All of these opportunities are Spirit-born and Spirit-led. God is the one who sustains me as long as I stay in step with His yoke of grace and the tempo He sets for my life.

As you begin to live out your new rhythms of grace, new opportunities will undoubtedly come your way. Before saying yes, the fundamental question to start with is: *What is God's purpose for me right now?* If you can sing, write, speak, teach, or serve others, that's great. But remember that, like a job, gifts are just the means; it's what's behind the gift or the ability that's important. Purpose isn't your gift, but your gifts can be an indicator of your purpose. How are you using those gifts? And in whom or what are you called to invest by means of your gifts? Like Jesus, if we are living for the eternal, the answers to these questions will always be connected to the difference we make in the lives of people.[11]

Preparation

Your preparation is the diligence you apply to cultivating your gifts and talents through education, training, and resources. If you don't invest in preparation, your opportunities will always be defined by your limited knowledge, experience, and skills. Preparation typically takes place behind the scenes and without much acknowledgment. We make mistakes and learn lessons—

sometimes hard and embarrassing ones. It's not the most exciting or glamorous aspect of the journey, and it's tempting to try to step around the process to get to the "good" parts. But preparation does more than give us a chance to hone our skills. The patient, obedient endurance we develop during preparation strengthens our character so it will be able to bear the weight of growth and opportunities yet to come. The apostle James writes, "Let perseverance finish its work so that you may be mature and complete, not lacking anything" (James 1:4).

There's a tension during the season of preparation: you might feel you have completed a season of preparation, but you haven't yet been given opportunities to use your gifts and skills. Let me encourage you to stay in this place. Don't try to force new opportunities if they aren't happening. As you continue to develop your gifts and skills, God will undoubtedly bring opportunities your way — opportunities that are just the right size to stretch your abilities and strengthen your character.

Positioning

Your positioning is the commitment you make to where God has placed you. The wisdom writer says, "Prepare your work outside; get everything ready for yourself in the field, and after that build your house" (Proverbs 24:27 ESV). This verse affirms that there is a practical, commonsense way to approach anything we build. Prepare your work, get the field ready, and *then* build your house. No one would build a house just by walking out to a plot of land and pouring concrete. That's not how the process works. The ground has to be prepared, leveled, and compacted. Buildings are permanent structures that need to be grounded in the right place. For the believer, that place is the context of the local church. Your purpose — the house you are called to build — isn't meant to be in some random spot all by itself. It is designed to be firmly established on the rock of Jesus Christ and positioned within the field of the local church.

Putting It All Together

Esther, one of the heroines of the Bible, offers a perfect example of how purpose, preparation, and positioning come together to create a fruitful opportunity worth investing in. Esther was a young Jewish girl who won the favor of King Ahasuerus and became his queen. When she learns of a plot to destroy all the Jews, she is presented an opportunity to rescue them by advocating on their behalf with the king. But it's literally a life-threatening opportunity — anyone who enters the king's inner court without being summoned and received by the king is put to death.

Queen Esther initially hesitates, knowing her life is at risk. But her cousin Mordecai reminds Esther of her greater purpose: "For if you keep silent at this time, relief and deliverance will rise for the Jews from another place, but you and your father's house will perish. And who knows whether you have not come to the kingdom *for such a time as this*?" (Esther 4:14 ESV, emphasis added). Mordecai's declaration of "such a time as this" acknowledges Esther's purpose at this time in her life — to save the Jews.

Queen Esther then prepared herself for her visit to the king. She refrained from eating and drinking for three days and asked all the Jews in Susa to do the same. On the third day, Esther presented herself before the king. He not only preserved her life, but accepted Esther's invitation to a banquet feast she had prepared for him and Haman, the villain who was plotting to kill the Jews. Esther won the king's favor and eventually exposed Haman's plot. The king intervened, Haman was executed, and the Jews were saved from destruction.

Esther recognized her purpose in this opportunity; she was diligent in the preparation process; and she strategically positioned herself in the presence of the king. It was a great risk, but it bore tremendous fruit. Esther played a role in a much larger story. Saving the Jewish people allowed the story of God's saving work in and through Abraham's descendants to come to pass. This is how we have salvation through Christ and the gospel. Esther seized a huge opportunity with eternal rewards that have continued to this day, and will continue for generations to come.

Esther shows us that these three P's can fit together in a sequence, in a process. Where are you in the process right now? Are you in a season of discovering your purpose? A season of preparation and hidden development? Are you struggling to stay in the place God has placed you? You might need to take the next step of committing yourself to being positioned to fulfill God's purpose. In every season, we may struggle with where God has us. No matter where we are in the process, it's important to stay in close fellowship with Him and allow Him to lead us into the next opportunity.

The Opportunity Evaluation Filter

In addition to the three P's, there is another helpful filter I use to help me discern the best opportunities. It's based on the woman described in Proverbs 31, who is an expert at seizing the right opportunities. How does she do it? First, notice what the Bible says:

> She considers a [new] field before she buys or accepts it [expanding prudently and not courting neglect of her present duties by assuming other duties]; with her savings [of time and strength] she plants fruitful vines in her vineyard. (Proverbs 31:16 AMP)

She considers. The word "consider" means to pause, reflect on, or examine. In other words, the woman who *considers* engages in some degree of "market research" before making a purchase. Perhaps you know someone like this. Before purchasing a washer or dryer, she will look up *Consumer Reports* online, or Google her top five models so she can read all the customer reviews. She'll want to know how many towels she can cram in all at once, while at the same time evaluating how energy efficient it is. Or how quickly it will dry fifteen pairs of jeans without sounding like an airplane is landing in her washroom. *She considers.* This is not a hasty woman, jumping at any opportunity that comes her way. She's deliberate and calculated, and by the time she's ready to make a decision, she'll be an expert on what the market offers.

In the same way, we need to carefully consider new opportunities that could potentially change the pace of our lives. If we choose to proceed, we must do so from a position of well-informed strength. So what are some of the questions we need to consider? Here are a few to use as a starting point:

- How closely does this opportunity align with my purpose?
- What value will it add to my life and the lives of those I love?
- What kind of time commitment will this opportunity require of me?
- Is this opportunity something that is already achieving results, or will it require significant investment up front in order to eventually be fruitful or worthwhile?
- Is it a short-term win, or is it a long-term investment that might not show its true value for years to come?

How you answer these questions should clarify the amount of time, energy, and resources you'll need to invest if you move ahead and say yes. There may be additional questions you'll need to ask based on the opportunity. The key is taking the time to pause and prayerfully *consider*.

She does not neglect her present duties. New opportunities are not an exit strategy from present responsibilities. When we consider beforehand, we need to make sure saying yes won't prevent us from stewarding other fields God has entrusted into our care. Within every yes to one thing, there is an inherent no to another. So we must consider ahead of time what we will, in fact, be saying no to if we accept this opportunity.

For example, I may be offered an opportunity that looks really good until I consider the time, energy, or financial requirements. Because I already have responsibilities and obligations, I have to consider how saying yes will impact my ability to keep those commitments. How will saying yes affect my family? Will it deplete me so much that I come home at the end of each day with nothing left to give? Will the money I make be more than the money I spend to pursue this opportunity? Will it uproot me and cause me to leave behind friendships and influence that have taken years to build?

By considering the new opportunity in light of current responsibilities, I may discern that the opportunity is a good one, but perhaps the timing is not right. God usually begins to prompt me about transitions and changes long before they actually need to take place. Maybe you've experienced the same thing. Just because we feel a tugging toward a new opportunity doesn't mean that the time is right. Here are some additional questions to consider:

- How will this opportunity impact my ability to meet my current obligations and responsibilities?

- What will I need to say no to in order to say yes to this?

- Am I currently strong enough and skilled enough to meet

the demands of this opportunity, or do I need to invest some time in preparation to do this well?

- If the opportunity is job related, is there someone else who could care for the responsibilities I currently have? If not, how can I find, equip, and transition such a person to take my place?

Before we reach out for new opportunities, we must consider our current responsibilities. If the fit or the timing is not right, we wait. We will never regret waiting, but we will likely regret jumping into something that compromises the commitments we already have.

She is focused on fruitfulness. The woman in Proverbs 31 "plants fruitful vines." When she buys the new field, it doesn't bankrupt her; she has margin in both time and resources. She doesn't come to the field with nothing left. She is prepared for a new season of growth!

So what exactly is fruitfulness in our context? Perhaps it's best first to identify what fruitfulness is not—it's not busyness, acclaim, or profit. Fruitfulness is what happens when we do the will of the Father. It's about *shalom*, not maximizing our schedule. It's about peace, not financial gain. It means I'm not just doing something because I can, but because it will add to the bigger picture in my life. Fruitfulness comes from personal wholeness; it's an expression of *shalom*. It answers yes to this question: Does this bring wholeness to my life?

In being a pastor to women, I have found that lack of fruitfulness is one of the greatest causes of frustration and a sense of purposelessness. I've met so many women who say their days are filled with activity, yet they don't experience a fruitful return. In other words, they don't feel like they are seeing any results from their investments of time and effort. They might be laboring on projects or relationships, but they feel like they aren't getting anywhere and the future seems bleak and without any opportunities for growth or change.

Part of the reason these women are not making progress may be what they bring—or don't bring—into the new opportunity. When we step into an opportunity, we shouldn't enter empty-handed. We need to prepare and pace ourselves to go the distance by storing up reserves. If we prepare for the long run, we will be able to bring strength into each new opportunity. We can finish one season strong and enter the next with reserves.

The wise woman from Proverbs 31 thinks ahead to what will happen when her vineyard becomes increasingly fruitful. She understands that if she invests wisely and stewards this field well, the natural outcome will be increase. A grower expects growth, and she is prepared for it. In fact, growth is her goal. She's not surprised when it happens; she then finds a new field and the process begins again!

If we are growing—that is, if we are good stewards of the opportunities God has entrusted to us—the chances are good that we will experience new opportunities for growth and increased fruitfulness. The more we bear fruit, the more God entrusts us with. Therefore, we must be prepared to welcome it when it comes.

Just as fruit has its seasons—time for sowing, time for bearing fruit, time of pruning, and time of dormancy—our lives have cycles of fruitfulness. Recognize what season you're in and be prepared for the next. With any new opportunity, working through the evaluation filter takes time. You might know what you are supposed to do, yet feel uneasy because the timing is not right. Use this season of waiting to engage the "consideration" process. Focus on fruitfulness and make room for growth. And of course, we must always cover our consideration process with prayer. You will be amazed how the pieces fall into place when God's timing is right, and it will all be confirmed by His peace.

For Reflection

1. When you consider the three components of fruitful opportunities (pages 164–67), which do you relate to most right now—purpose, preparation, or positioning? Why?

2. If you are considering any specific opportunities right now, reflect on them using the opportunity evaluation filter (pages 169–73). What insights does this process provide?

3. What do you sense the Holy Spirit might be saying to you about your opportunities?

Chapter 12

Embrace Personal Wholeness

The integrity of the upright will guide them,
But the perversity of the unfaithful will destroy them.

Proverbs 11:3 NKJV

A life paced in rhythms of grace is an outward expression of an inner world that is healthy and whole. Our divine tempo over-flows from an inner state of *shalom*, so it stands to reason that our inner condition has an impact on the rhythm of our lives. This is personal wholeness. By personal wholeness, I mean emotional and mental wholeness. It is the degree of freedom we have from things like shame, rejection, insecurity, fear, and anything else that undermines us from the inside out. We need this kind of inner fortitude in order to make the necessary decisions and to set the necessary boundaries that enable us to live according to these rhythms. To get a clearer picture of what it means to make decisions and set boundaries from a place of wholeness, consider the following scenarios and see if any of them feel familiar.

- Some of Sarah's extended family members pass through town unexpectedly and invite her to join them for dinner. She really wants to connect with them, but she already has plans to attend a going-away party for a good friend who is moving to another state. She says yes to her family out of a sense of obligation, but all through dinner she regrets disappointing her friend. Nevertheless, she smiles politely and participates in the conversation without betraying her true feelings.

- Nina's boss asks her to attend a work function that overlaps with her son's opening soccer game of the season. She knows this is an important game, but agrees to participate because the annual performance reviews are coming up and she is up for a promotion. If the function ends on time, she should at least be able to make it to the second half of the game. But the function drags on, and Nina looks at her watch only to realize that her son's game will soon be over. She looks down at her phone and pretends to read an email so no one at the table will notice the tears welling up in her eyes. This game was so important to her son—she can't believe she missed it!

- Barb has been going nonstop for the last three weeks. Her mother fractured her hip and needed extra care every day last week. The week before that, her sister-in-law and her four children spent spring break in her cramped guest room. And the week before that, she coordinated all the décor and food for her niece's wedding reception. Even though Barb loves helping others, she is ready for a break! This weekend she has nothing planned, and that thought kept her going through all the craziness. Just as Barb is settling in on Friday night, her teenage daughter walks through the front door with five giggling friends. "Hey, Mom! Shelly's parents decided to go out of town for their anniversary, so we're moving the prom committee sleepover to our house. Is that okay?" Barb gives in because she doesn't want to be a party-pooper, but later that night, she lies in bed fuming over her decision while pounding music, loud talking, and random crashing sounds echo down the hallway from her daughter's bedroom. *Why do I always give in?* she wonders.

This list of scenarios could go on — and I'm sure you could add a few more of your own! In each situation, the women were forced to make choices between conflicting values. Though they had already made decisions based on their commitments, priorities, and desires, they were easily swayed by new opportunities and responsibilities that challenged those decisions. Neither Sarah, Nina, nor Barb changed course because they thought it was the best thing or the right thing to do. There were other factors at work. Sarah's sense of responsibility to her family conflicted with her loyalty to her friend. Nina's priority of family conflicted with her career goals and opportunities. Barb's legitimate need for rest conflicted with her desire to be a supportive and loving parent. But in each case, the choices they made resulted in a gap between what each woman felt on the inside and what she communicated to others on the outside.

We have all been in this kind of situation at one time or another, haven't we? I know I have. I have given in to pressure and made choices I knew would come back to bite me in the end. I simply did not have the maturity and strength to make choices that aligned with my convictions and values. Sure enough, I always ended up divided — portraying happiness on the outside while on the inside I was struggling with disappointment, regret, or anger.

Part of establishing and sustaining rhythms of grace is closing the gap between our inner reality and our outer behavior. This does not mean our goal is to achieve perfection. It means we make a lifetime commitment to becoming the same person on the outside that we are on the inside. That is, we make a commitment to being people of integrity.

The Wholeness of Integrity

The word "integrity" comes from the word "integer." An integer is simply a whole number, a number without fractions. God is perfect in His wholeness and therefore in His integrity. The apostle James says it this way: "There is nothing deceitful in God, nothing two-faced, nothing fickle" (James 1:17 MSG). In other words, God has integrity—there is no gap between God's inner and outer worlds. They are the same.

We grow in personal wholeness, or integrity, by humbly living a lifestyle of obedience to God and setting our confidence in His grace. The first great commandment is, "You shall love the LORD your God with *all* your heart and with *all* your soul and with *all* your might" (Deuteronomy 6:5 ESV, emphasis added). The only fitting way to respond to the *one* God is by loving Him with our *all*. Our hearts, our souls, our might—whole, undivided, and unfractured—are the measure of our devotion to Him.

People with integrity are not perfect, but they are *whole*hearted—undivided in their beliefs and actions. The apostle James paints a picture of the double-minded person, which is the opposite of a person with integrity:

> If any of you lacks wisdom, you should ask God, who gives generously to all without finding fault, and it will be given to you. But when you ask, you must believe and not doubt, because the one who doubts is like a wave of the sea, blown

and tossed by the wind. That person should not expect to receive anything from the Lord. Such a person is double-minded and unstable in all they do. (James 1:5–8)

James doesn't mean our faith has to be perfect and free from doubt of any kind. What he warns against is not doubting whether God will give us wisdom, but against doubting the wisdom that God does give. We must not have a divided heart when we ask God for wisdom. A person with a divided heart approaches God's wisdom like someone writing to an advice column about a problem. They ask so they can weigh the advice they get there against other options. A person with a divided heart is not sure if she will obey God's wisdom; she just wants to see what God has to say before she decides one way or the other.

When we approach God this way, we're starting off on the wrong foot before we utter the first word in prayer. Double-minded people have two mind-sets. They are not whole, but fractured in their intentions to follow God. This is what makes them "unstable in all their ways," which is just another way of saying that someone lacks integrity or wholeness. When we think of people who lack integrity, we may imagine people who cheat, are habitual liars, or always break their promises. These are extreme examples, but they are rooted in a much less obvious source: a divided heart.

Some things that can cause us to have a divided heart include painful past experiences, conflicting desires, or fear. For example:

- You've started a new relationship and would like to pursue it further, but fear of rejection from a previous broken relationship holds you back. Your past experiences conflict with your hopes for the future you dream of.

- You have a desire to become fit and healthy, but you hate exercising and refuse to eat anything remotely like fruits and vegetables. Your desire for health conflicts with your desire to continue in unhealthy habits.

- A new business venture opens up to you. It sounds exciting and is just the opportunity you have been praying about and hoping for. But you hesitate to pursue it because you fear the risk involved. Your fear of failure keeps you from having the career you believe is right for you.

We can also experience a divided heart when there is a gap between inner and outer worlds. Just as in the examples at the beginning of the chapter about Sarah, Nina, and Barb, we experience a disconnect between who we are on the inside and what we express on the outside.

May I be totally honest and say that I have lived with a divided heart for way too long? Over the years, I have had many different roles to fulfill, and many goals related to each of those roles. As a result, I also had many different measures of success that sometimes seemed to be in competition with each other. At home, success meant nurturing my children and respecting my husband. But at work, success meant being a bold decision maker and a fearless leader. Those are two very different expressions of "success." Over time, I began to feel as if I was breaking apart from the inside out.

To complicate matters, the private me, my core personality, is an introverted intellectual. I'm constantly lost in my thoughts like an absentminded professor—and I like it there! I could sit in the quiet for hours just pondering the mysteries of the universe. I can be completely happy without talking to anyone for long periods of time. Needless to say, ministry is at the top of the list of careers I probably should *not* enter. Of course, I didn't know that when I entered ministry. Yet in spite of the many ways that ministry may not fit the perfect career profile for a person like me, I know this is where I belong. Nevertheless, for many years there was a gap between who I was in my natural state and who I felt I needed to be in order to fulfill the demands of my ministry role.

To deal with my frustration about feeling inadequate, I developed this convincing but unwise little habit. I called it "putting on my game face." When I left the serenity of my private world each day to step into my challenging, outer world of ministry, I shut down that part of me that needs solace and quiet, and then I psyched up the part of myself that was more people-oriented. In this way, I skipped over the little gap that separated my private self from my public self, and I poured every ounce of emotional and relational energy I had into my work. By the time I came home at the end of each day, I was completely drained. I hopped back over that little gap into my private world and collapsed on the couch.

Maybe this doesn't seem like a big deal to you. You're probably thinking, *Isn't that what we are supposed to do each day when we get home from work? Aren't we supposed to crash and relax so we can recharge for the next day?* Those are good points. But the problem wasn't that I was relaxing and recharging each evening. It was that I was hopping back and forth between two different versions of myself. The longer I kept hopping, the wider the gap got. Eventually, I couldn't make the jump anymore.

To some extent, all of us have a gap between our inner and outer worlds. While it's healthy to have some degree of separation between our private and public lives, there should also be a basic alignment between the two. What is visible on the outside might not reveal every detail of our inner landscape, but neither should it be an entirely different picture. For years, I considered my natural personality a limitation to my ministry "performance." I thought of it as something I had to overcome or deny in order to be productive. Instead of accepting who I truly was and trusting in the sufficiency of Christ's grace to make up what was lacking, as I do now, I tried to act like the kind of person I thought I should be, not the person I really was. That's a divided heart, plain and simple. I've had to learn the hard way that to truly lead a life of wholeness, I must have complete dependence on God's sufficiency, not my own. And this means starting from a place of personal honesty.

Personal Honesty

My one big rule when it comes to building a life of integrity is personal honesty. Making a commitment to personal honesty helps me close the gap between my inner and outer worlds. That might seem like a pretty obvious way to understand integrity, but it wasn't always how I understood it. You see, I used to think about personal integrity as code for "don't compromise your witness." *Don't lie, because Christians don't do that, and you don't want to "compromise your witness." Don't get drunk or cuss, because Christians don't do those things either, and you wouldn't want to "compromise your witness."* If we want to be people of integrity, the question we should be asking is not, "What rules should I follow to guard my witness?" but, "What kind of person do I want to be?"

What kind of person do you want to be? I can tell you some of the things I want to be. I want to be truthful, loyal, dependable, kind, generous, merciful, humble, hard-working, and positive. Integrity keeps my desires to be this kind of person — my inner world — in alignment with my outer world. That means:

- I don't tell the truth just to be a good Christian. I tell the truth because I want to be truthful. Liars lie, and I don't want to be a liar.

- I tithe and give offerings as an expression of my trust in God. I give because I want to be generous. Stingy people refuse to give, and I don't want to be stingy.

- I refrain from gossiping about my friends not because I want everyone to think I'm super spiritual and holy. I refrain from gossip because I want to be a loyal person. Backstabbers gossip, and I don't want to be a backstabber.

Once we decide what kind of person we want to be, growing in integrity becomes less about conforming to a list of behaviors and more about the process of becoming whole, reconciling our inner and outer worlds. The next thing to do is put our commitment to personal honesty into action in four key areas—our speech, our shortcomings, our limits and boundaries, and our motives.

Honesty in Our Speech

Our words are a great place to start when it comes to building a life of integrity. Personal honesty in speech means I say what I mean and I truly mean what I say. Jesus tells us to "let your 'Yes' be 'Yes,' and your 'No,' 'No'" (Matthew 5:37 NKJV). When we are honest, our words are simple and sincere. When we compliment someone, we really mean it—no strings attached. When we are unhappy with a situation, we are honest in our communication about it, without fluff and without harshness.

How many times have we used flattery to manipulate people into doing what we want them to do or giving something we want? How often have we stretched the truth to avoid having a difficult conversation? Or we told a partial truth to avoid the consequences of our actions? Most of the time when we're dishonest with our speech, it's because we're afraid of what will happen if we tell the truth. We might fear another person's response, the consequences of the truth coming to light, or simply being vulnerable. The key thing to ask yourself is: *What in my heart is preventing me from telling the truth?* Personal honesty means not just stopping the behavior but fixing the root cause. Addressing the root cause of dishonesty enables us to speak and live with integrity.

Honesty about Our Shortcomings

You were wrong, you dropped the ball, you made a mistake. It happens! But it can be so hard to admit it, right? Yet, one of the marks of wholeness is the ability to take responsibility for mistakes and failures. It is rare to find a model example of someone taking personal responsibility. We hear a lot today about politicians, business leaders, and even pastors who avoid taking true responsibility for mistakes that are highly unethical and sooner or later tend to become public. It's easy to acknowledge vaguely that something unfortunate happened, but rarely do we hear someone plainly admit they are at fault.

Being committed to personal honesty about your shortcomings means you acknowledge you are human. You admit you have flaws and make mistakes and you own up to them. For example:

- You failed your last exam — not because the professor is too harsh but because you procrastinated and didn't study until the night before.

- Your kids and spouse have been irritated with you recently — not because they are moody and intent on making your life miserable, but because you have been doing overtime at work and not spending enough time with them.

- A friend of yours is no longer on speaking terms with you — not because you both are just too busy but because you gossiped about your friend and it got back to her. Now she feels betrayed.

We all have our own shortcomings and make mistakes; we simply need to be honest about them and make amends. A person who has difficulty readily admitting they are wrong or saying they are sorry will not be able to consistently experience *shalom* and grow in wholeness.

Honesty about Our Limits and Boundaries

Being honest about our limits and boundaries means recognizing what we can and can't do—and sticking to it. Most of us know we have personal limits, so why is it so difficult to accept them and be honest with ourselves and others when we reach these limits?

Most of us who call ourselves believers have a strong conviction about treating others with care and respect (or at least we should!). Our love for others—our families, our dear friends—prevents us from pushing them beyond reasonable limits. We would never knowingly or purposefully drive our children to exhaustion or our friends to the point of emotional breakdown. If someone we love expresses their limits, we respect those limits. Yet it's often difficult to honor similar limits for ourselves.

We all have limited resources—whether it's energy, time, physical endurance, or emotional capacity. The key is to recognize our limits and honor them—in both word and action. If we fail to do so, we undermine our integrity. Consider a few examples.

- If you tell your colleagues you can't meet a deadline without a two-week lead time, but then consistently give in to pressures to do it faster and work crazy amounts of overtime to meet the deadline in one week, you are being dishonest. Saying you need two weeks but finishing in one week is the same as saying, "I really just need one week." If you need two full weeks for completion, say two weeks and stick to it. Don't undermine your boundaries or disregard your limitations.

- You have a friend who is constantly in crisis. You want to offer encouragement and support, but it can be emotionally draining and you can't sustain the day-to-day drama in hour-long phone calls. You've asked to set up a specific time each week to connect and support your friend, but she continues to call at other times too—and you always take the call. To honor your limits, you need to set relational boundaries in your friendship and stick to them.

- Your kids are asking for certain privileges—like upgraded cell phones—because all of their friends have the latest model. The technology upgrade certainly isn't necessary and the family budget certainly doesn't allow for it, but you don't want to be the stingy mom who always says no. So you agree that you'll "talk to Dad about it" even though you know that you need to say no. Your integrity just took a hit.

Knowing your limits and sticking to your boundaries is an essential part of personal wholeness.

Honesty about Our Motives

It's incredibly important to assess the *why* behind what you do:

- *Why* is it so important to me to be included in that group of friends?

- *Why* do I keep saying yes even though I know I should say no?

- *Why* am I avoiding that conversation I've been meaning to have for weeks?

- *Why* am I screening calls from that person?

If we can gather the courage to be brutally honest with ourselves about the *whys*—our motives—it will help us continue along the path of integrity. Far too often, however, we may not even know ourselves why we do the things we do. Taking some time to assess our motives, even if we find them unpleasant, and then acknowledging that motive (at least to ourselves) will push us along the path to personal honesty and integrity.

When we are dishonest with ourselves to avoid conflict, we enlarge the gap between our inner and outer worlds and work against wholeness. We might feel at peace with everyone around us because we avoided a fight, but we create conflict within ourselves when we aren't being true to who we are. Or conversely, we might be at peace with ourselves because we did exactly what we wanted to do, but doing so resulted in conflict with others. A commitment to personal honesty and honesty with others bridges the gap between our inner and outer worlds.

The Grace of Wholeness

A wholehearted commitment to personal honesty requires tremendous courage and faith. We can only accomplish that fully by relying on the grace of God. The wholeness of His grace—His acceptance, love, and power for living—is the only thing that can give us the courage to live in a way that is so contrary to the system of this world.

Personal wholeness means trusting that God's wonderful grace is just enough for you. His grace releases us from the pressures of perfect performance. When we admit we are not perfect and never can be, we declare that God is perfect and everything about Him—His work, timing, strength, provision—is perfect as well. We don't have to try to be someone we're not and we can be completely honest about our weaknesses. When I am under the yoke of grace, I am content with where I am right here, right now, weakness and all ... as long as I am walking close to Jesus.

Personal wholeness is not just an outcome (something we

might treat as a project), but also the sustainer of a lifetime of living for and with God (which is a process rooted in a relationship). All the good intentions and pacesetting changes we make will have limited or short-lived results if we are not simultaneously allowing God to change us from the inside out. While we are making room for Sabbath rest, prioritizing our relationships and health, and making wise decisions about our opportunities, we must also remember to let God do a true transforming work in our hearts. We do this through a lifestyle of humble submission and obedience to Him.

We won't experience the fullness of *shalom*—personal wholeness in its most perfect form—until we get to heaven, but right now we are moving, as the Bible says, "from glory to glory" (2 Corinthians 3:18 NKJV). We are all at different places. I'm further along than I was a couple years ago, but I still have a long way to go. I still sometimes get out of step because I am insecure over how people might perceive me or afraid of failing to meet their expectations. But after being in step with God's rhythm, I can recognize my fears more quickly now, and it's easier to get back into the right tempo. The more we grow in personal wholeness, the more it will overflow into the rest of our lives and the easier it will be to move to the rhythms of grace, the beat of heaven's drum.

For Reflection

1. Briefly recall a recent situation when you agreed to something you knew you would regret later. How would you describe the split between your inner life and your outer life in that situation?

2. When you consider the various components of personal honesty (pages 182–87), which would you say you struggle with most? In what ways does this lack of honesty keep you from experiencing wholeness?

3. What do you sense the Holy Spirit might be saying to you about personal wholeness?

Chapter 13

Keep the Pace

*Keep your eyes on Jesus, who both began
and finished this race we're in.*

Hebrews 12:2 MSG

There was nothing to do but wait. I had just taken the most intense bathroom break of my life. As I sat on the side of the bathtub, I gazed attentively at the tiny windows on the pregnancy test wand I was holding in my hand. In the minute or so that passed, feelings of excitement and joy surged through me. The timer bell went off and a tiny little line that didn't exist a few seconds ago was now staring me in the face confirming what I already suspected to be true. We were going to have our first baby!

Like most first-time moms, I embraced most of my pregnancy with enthusiasm. The joy over the miraculous little being growing inside me was even enough to make the morning sickness and fatigue seem worthwhile. I spent the first few months joyfully sharing the news with friends. Then as my due date drew closer, I began buying pink baby clothes and decorating the nursery. I was so ready to meet my baby girl that I used to lay her little nighties in the crib and stand there looking down at them, imagining what she would look like sleeping angelically through the night. (That "through the night" part was definitely prenatal fantasy!)

But in the third trimester, my patience started to wear thin. I was tired of misjudging the angle of the extra-wide turns required by my new, ahem, "voluptuous" figure and bumping into tables and doorframes. I was sick of people—some of them total strangers—rubbing my belly like a magic eight ball and making comments about my weight. But more than any of these things, I was just tired of waiting.

When in the world is this baby going to get here? Of course, I didn't need to wonder at all. I had a due date. I knew what it was. My doctor gave it to me on my first visit. I just wondered if she might be wrong. I found myself asking, "Are you sure you calculated the right due date?" Not that I wanted the baby to come early—certainly not. It's just that I was so uncomfortable and, well, *over* it. But even though I was "so over" being pregnant, the process of growth and development that had to take place for a healthy baby to be born wasn't finished.

Some things just can't be rushed, and growing a baby is one of those things. My own discomfort and impatience had absolutely no impact on the pace of that tiny baby's development. It takes forty weeks to grow a healthy, fully formed baby, and that's that. No amount of faith, or trying, or believing can change that. There is no way to circumvent or cut short the process. You can't pay to get your baby a fast pass, no preferred customer short line. Every baby in every body ideally percolates for forty weeks before puncturing the atmosphere of the delivery room with the first of many cries. There was nothing I could do but rest, relax, and enjoy the process.

Even as you read through the final pages of this book and come to the end of our journey together, you are just starting the process of recalibrating your personal world to reflect the wholeness and peace that come from matching your steps with God's tempo for your life. And just like I was in the early stages of my pregnancy, you might feel excited and full of anticipation about all the great changes lying ahead of you. That's a great way to start! But we also need to be honest. Those initial feelings of excitement won't last. They never do; it's just human nature.

As time goes on, you might start to feel like you aren't seeing the results you wanted to see. You might feel frustrated at times when you slip back into a reactive way of living and find yourself driven at a frantic and overwhelming pace. You might feel depressed when you give in to pressure and agree to things that, in hindsight, are clearly not the best choice for you at the moment. Those times will happen — and it's okay. They happen to me, too. I'm not anywhere close to perfect when it comes to walking in the rhythms of grace. I get out of step from time to time. That's when I remind myself that this is a process — a lifelong process — that is covered by grace. Just as I had to learn to enjoy the process of growing a baby for forty weeks without rushing or shortcuts, I have to learn to enjoy the process of spiritual and personal growth.

Enjoying the process means I am free from performance anxiety. What is beautiful in its time is also perfectly appropriate for its time. When the day finally arrived for Stovall and me to meet our beautiful firstborn, she was absolutely perfect and complete, nothing lacking. She was a perfectly mature *baby*. That's not to say she was perfectly mature. She didn't come out walking and talking and doing algebra. That wouldn't be beautiful at all — it would be totally weird. But for that moment, at that time, she was perfect. She was everything she needed to be and everything I could possibly wish for her to be *right then*. Maturity doesn't mean that we have made it to perfection or that we will never have to change again. It means that we are right where we need to be for now, and we are free to enjoy our current season of life without shame about our shortcomings or pressure to perform better.

It also means we don't become so focused on where we are headed that we forget something beautiful is being formed and developed in us. The pace of grace is not hurried, but measured. Scripture affirms that God "has made everything beautiful in its time. He has also set eternity in the human heart; yet no one can fathom what God has done from beginning to end" (Ecclesiastes 3:11). My baby needed a full nine months to grow, and despite my discomfort in the process, God's perfect timing was at work. Excitement and zeal are great motivators to jolt us into starting something new, but patience and perseverance are what bring us across the finish line. Our job is not to hurry ahead to the goal, but to match our steps to God's tempo. We do that by pacing ourselves now to run the full distance.

Running the Full Distance

Metaphors can only take us so far, and in case you missed it, I just changed the one we're working with. The Christian life is like a race, which is a perfect picture for what we're talking about here.

Pacing ourselves is an art, not a science or a discipline. When you talk to long-distance runners, they will tell you that proper pacing is not a formulaic process a runner can learn and then do perfectly every time she runs. That's not to say there aren't scientific formulas about how to achieve and maintain the optimal long-distance pacing—there is plenty of science on that topic. But when it comes down to putting it into practice, to shoes hitting the dirt, the runner doesn't rely on scientific formulas. She relies on intuition, a zone she hits. And she just knows. *This is it. This is good. This is the perfect pace for right now.*

When this happens, we say a runner has "hit her stride." Body, terrain, and focus all come into alignment. The rhythm of her feet hitting the ground, the beating of her heart, the cadence of her stride all converge to create a momentum that seems greater than just "miles per hour." It's almost like the ground itself is pushing her forward, willing her to go farther, lending her its strength. This moment, this zone, is why runners run.

When a runner hits her stride, the last thing she wants to do is break it, but keeping her pace is a lot harder than it seems. A runner can break her pace, even by running a few seconds per mile too fast, which can set her up for fatigue, loss of drive, and even injury later on in the race. Because of this, every long-distance runner has to master the art of pacing. Those who finish well understand the necessity of pacing themselves for the long run. If we want to run the race of this life with endurance and finish it well, the same principle applies to us. We must learn to pace ourselves from start to finish.

Let's take a look at four key running tips for keeping the pace, each of which reveals truths that can help us keep a steady pace for the long haul in our own lives.

Be in tune with your body. A runner must have a solid sense and innate knowledge of the fastest pace she can sustain through the full race distance. In other words, she has to begin her race with a clear view of the finish line and understand what it will take to finish. She also needs to be sufficiently in tune with her body to adjust her pace along the way based on how she feels. If the runner's mind begins to wander and she stops paying attention to how her body is feeling and responding, she can modify her pace without realizing it. She might not realize her heart is beating too fast or too slow or that the cadence of her stride has increased or decreased. She has to be in tune with her body to recognize small changes that reflect a need to adjust her pace.

In the same way, you and I need to be in tune with our bodies. If you are constantly tired and fatigued, maybe your pace has gotten a little too fast. If you are not able to keep up with your normal activities, maybe a poor diet or lack of sleep is the culprit. It's too easy to ignore our bodies until they give out on us, and we wind up sick in bed or set back by something more serious. I used to push myself even when I knew I was getting sick. I went into the office to meet a deadline and attend meetings (and spread my germs, to my coworkers' dismay). I thought I just needed to toughen up, medicate, and press through. But after a few days of doing that, I was on my back for a week missing even more work. Now I have learned that when I sense sickness coming on, I need to stop and rest. Then, instead of being out of the game for a week, I am usually down for about two days. Instead of rushing ahead to meet deadlines no matter what the cost, I pace myself. Usually the time difference isn't anything substantial.

Don't let positive momentum fool you. Believe it or not, maintaining a measured pace when you would rather run faster is often more difficult than speeding up a pace that has become too slow. Remember how we described a runner who has hit her stride? The positive energy and momentum she feels in that zone do not reflect her abilities or capacity. It is a temporary state of optimum performance that is the by-product of everything in her body and her environment being perfectly in sync. It will not last forever. She knows this intellectually, but in the moment, when everything is working together, she feels more powerful than she really is. At the height of her performance, then, she is most vulnerable to breaking the rhythm of her pace by speeding up. If she does, she may make a momentary gain, but she will fall behind where it counts … in the final leg.

When you get into a great rhythm, be aware that this can be one of your most vulnerable times. When you "hit your stride," it's typical for opportunities to come flying your way, perhaps even some you have been hoping and praying about for a long time. The momentum and energy of everything in your life working and moving in perfect rhythm can make you feel invincible. Don't forget, you're not invincible. "The zone" is a temporary state. It won't last forever, and it's not meant to. But if you pace yourself well, it will come again.

Know your personal cadence. A runner's pace is measured by how many strides she takes per minute. This is called a runner's cadence. The cadence of each runner is unique and influenced by several factors. These include the runner's fitness level, level of training, experience as a runner, and aspects of her body shape, such as the length of her legs. All of these play a part in setting the cadence for a pace that is right for her.

Just like a runner, you have a cadence that is unique and perfectly suited to you so you can finish the race marked out for you. Your life, like each stage of a long-distance race, requires different tempos at different stages. Sometimes you have to go pretty fast in order to stay on pace. There are seasons when you might have to work harder than usual, but you know it is only for a short time. There are other times when you feel like you might have hit the "cruise control" button of your life—things just seem to be moving along at a pretty easy and sustainable pace. You are running and keeping up, but it is not at an over-the-top pace. We adjust the tempo of our pace to the stages of our life, just like a runner adjusts her pace to certain stages of the race.

To run with endurance and finish your race well, you must be aware not only of your cadence, but also of the pace required for the leg you are running right now. One stride does not—and should not—fit all. When you match the cadence of your pace to the stage of the race you are running, you will find your divine tempo, your rhythms of grace, and you will hit your stride!

Don't let distractions derail you. The most important aspect of pace training is for the runner to discipline herself to stick to the winning pace no matter how she feels—whether she has a burst of energy and wants to run faster to make better time, or whether she feels her energy lagging and she begins to wonder if she can make it to the finish line. *Keep the pace.* If she is bored with the route she has run countless times by now, the challenge remains: *keep the pace.*

The same challenge lies ahead of you as you begin to run your next leg of the race, now paced by grace and set to the rhythms of God's divine tempo. You recognize the importance of being patient with yourself and trusting in God's perfect timing. All the same, distractions will come.

- The energy and momentum of success can be distractions. When you are bursting with energy and want to run ahead, *keep the pace.*

- Discouragement and disappointment can be distractions. When your energy and optimism lag and you wonder if you should just stop running, *keep the pace.*

- Boredom and monotony can be distractions. When you are bored with your usual route and are tempted to hurry ahead, *keep the pace.*

- Uncertainty and worry can be distractions. When you are not sure what to do next and you feel a little lost and insecure, *keep the pace.*

Ultimately, keeping the pace is about focus. That's why the writer of Hebrews urges us to "keep your eyes on Jesus, who both began and finished this race we're in. Study how he did it. Because he never lost sight of where he was headed—that exhilarating finish in and with God" (Hebrews 12:2 MSG).

Navigating the Path Ahead

There will always be times when our next steps are not certain and the path ahead is not clear. It's at these times we need to be more in tune than ever with the voice of the Holy Spirit and more in step than ever with the rhythms of grace. Most of us will never have a detailed map of every twist and turn along the trail of life. That's because God's navigation system isn't based on *seeing*; it's based on *hearing*. We have a vivid example of this in Jesus' last conversations with His disciples.

At the Last Supper, Jesus told them, "There is so much more I want to tell you, but you can't bear it now" (John 16:12 NLT). It's easy to gloss over those words, but we need to remember that Jesus had just dropped a bomb on His closest followers. He told them He was leaving them and that His kingdom would not be of this world. In addition to grappling with the reality of Jesus' impending death, they were also coming to grips with some pretty ominous predictions about their own fate. And then Jesus basically says, "I have more details about this whole plan, but you're not ready to hear them now. So you will just have to wait and find out later." *Um, excuse me, Jesus, but didn't You just say You wouldn't be around later? Don't You think, like,* right now *would be the best time to lay out this whole plan to us?*

The disciples no doubt thought this "waiting for the plan" business was a bad idea. Yet, Jesus was okay with it because He knew the Holy Spirit would come and guide them into all truth (John 16:13). Jesus knew that if the disciples could just learn one thing—to listen to the Holy Spirit and obey—the Holy Spirit would help them with every obstacle they would face for the rest of their lives.

Hearing the voice of the Spirit, even though we do not have a detailed map of where our path will take us, was and still is

God's perfect navigation plan. The solution to the chaos in our lives is found in a sound—the sound of God's voice, speaking to us through the leading of the Holy Spirit. Just as God spoke order into chaos and brought forth creation, His voice can and will bring order into the chaos of your life as you listen closely to the Spirit and step into the rhythms of grace.

For Reflection

1. What stood out most to you about the teaching in this chapter? What do you sense the Holy Spirit might be saying to you?

2. As you consider your next steps and what will be required to begin living in rhythms of grace, what do you need from God? How do you need Him to help you?

3. What is your greatest take-away from reading this book?

Additional Resources

Ruth Haley Barton and Dallas Willard. *Invitation to Solitude and Silence: Experiencing God's Transforming Presence.* Downers Grove, IL: InterVarsity Press, 2010.

Ruth Haley Barton. *Sacred Rhythms: Arranging Our Lives for Spiritual Transformation.* Downers Grove, IL: InterVarsity Press, 2006.

Dietrich Bonhoeffer. *Psalms: The Prayer Book of the Bible.* Minneapolis: Augsburg Fortress, 1974.

Adele Ahlberg Calhoun. *Spiritual Disciplines Handbook: Practices that Transform Us.* Downers Grove, IL: InterVarsity Press, 2005.

Kristen Feola. *The Ultimate Guide to the Daniel Fast.* Grand Rapids: Zondervan, 2010.

Richard J. Foster. *Celebration of Discipline: The Path to Spiritual Growth.* San Francisco: HarperSanFrancisco, 2002.

Jentezen Franklin. *Fasting: Opening the Door to a Deeper, More Intimate, More Powerful Relationship with God.* Lake Mary, FL: Charisma House, 2014.

Robert Gelinas. *The Mercy Prayer: The One Prayer Jesus Always Answers.* Nashville: Nelson, 2013.

Susan Gregory. *The Daniel Fast: Feed Your Soul, Strengthen Your Spirit, and Renew Your Body.* Carol Stream, IL: Tyndale, 2010.

Susan Gregory and Richard J. Bloomer. *The Daniel Cure: The Daniel Fast Way to Vibrant Health.* Grand Rapids: Zondervan, 2013.

John Ortberg. *The Life You've Always Wanted: Spiritual Disciplines for Ordinary People*. Grand Rapids: Zondervan, 2002.

John Ortberg. *Soul Keeping: Caring for the Most Important Part of You*. Grand Rapids: Zondervan, 2014.

James W. Sire. *Praying the Psalms of Jesus*. Downers Grove, IL: InterVarsity Press, 2007.

Rick Warren, Dr. Daniel Amen, and Dr. Mark Hyman. *The Daniel Plan: Forty Days to a Healthier Life*. Grand Rapids: Zondervan, 2013.

Stovall Weems. *Awakening: A New Approach to Faith, Fasting, and Spiritual Freedom*. Colorado Springs: Waterbrook, 2009.

Dallas Willard. *The Spirit of the Disciplines: Understanding How God Changes Lives*. New York: HarperOne, 1999.

Reboot Guide[12]

Before You Get Started

Building a new schedule is a process that takes time. You'll get the most benefit out of the reboot if you can step out of your routine schedule and devote a block of time to it.

If you can, I encourage you to get away for a weekend or a day and a half—for example, a Friday night through Saturday. This will allow sufficient time for you to rest, pray, and prepare yourself to engage the reboot. Although a night away is optimal, it is not required. If you can't get away overnight, then try taking one day—six to twelve hours. Make arrangements for the kids and go to a favorite, quiet spot where you will be free to focus without interruptions.

If taking a day away is still too much for your schedule right now, you could spread things out over a week or more, doing one step every day or two. I will caution you, however, that spreading it out too much may diminish your focus and cause you to lose momentum. So be kind to yourself and don't skimp on the time. I promise it will pay off!

Here are a few things you'll need:

- A blank calendar for the coming year (You can print out pages from your computer calendar if you don't want to buy a calendar.)[13]

- A pad of paper or a journal
- Six to eight 3 x 5 note cards (or 4 x 6 cards if you want more space to write)
- Something to write with (preferably a pencil because you may need to erase)
- Your existing calendar (paper, laptop, or tablet, etc.) with all of your known events and commitments documented
- This Reboot Guide

Once you've set aside the time and gathered what you need for the reboot, begin by seeking God in prayer. We know from Scripture that "we can make our plans, but the Lord determines our steps" (Proverbs 16:9 NLT). Surrender your desires to God, ask for his wisdom, and invite the Holy Spirit to lead you as you enter this planning process.

STEP 1: Identify Your Theme for the Year

A theme provides focus for the year. It might be something God wants to accomplish in your life, an area of your life that needs greater attention, or a way in which you want to stretch and grow.

Each chapter throughout *Rhythms of Grace* concluded with this question: "What do you sense the Holy Spirit might be saying to you about _____?" If you wrote down your responses to these questions, review them now to see if you can identify any common issues, words, or phrases. These may provide clues to help you identify your theme. For example, recurring issues related to working overtime and neglecting family might point toward a theme of *balance*. Phrases such as "always feeling tired," "can't ever get ahead," or "my mind can't stop running" might highlight a theme of *rest* for the year ahead. If you say you feel a sense of being disorganized or "all over the place," perhaps *structure* might be a good theme to consider.

If you weren't able to write down your responses at the end of the chapters, prayerfully consider what you sense the Holy Spirit is inviting you to pay attention to and prioritize in the year ahead.

In your journal or on a pad of paper, write down anything that stands out to you. If you have a strong sense of what your theme is, write it down: *My theme for the year is* _____.

If nothing stands out, keep working through the remaining steps and come back to consider your theme again later.

STEP 2: Get the Big-Picture Perspective

Getting the big picture helps you to identify where you are and where you want to be in the year ahead. The questions that follow are designed to help you get a handle on what's happening in your life right now, to name any changes that might be coming soon, and to identify any potential trade-offs you may need to make as you establish your new rhythm. Write responses in your journal or on a pad of paper.

- **What season of life are you currently in?** Your season of life includes not just your age but your personal and professional circumstances. For example: *I am a forty-something working mom of three kids. My children all live at home, but they are teenagers and pretty self-sufficient. My parents and in-laws are healthy and do not need special care. I am established and happy in my career and am not seeking a career change.*

- **What possible changes might you anticipate in the next six months?** These are things that you know could happen but aren't yet certain of. Keep them in mind as you may want to allow margin for them in your schedule. For example: *I might be moving if I can sell my house. I would like to serve on that community center board if I am invited. I would like to cut back on my hours at work over the summer if my boss is open to it.*

- **What do you know for sure you are supposed to be doing right now?** These are the events, projects, and commitments you are 100 percent certain are worthy of the space they take up in your life. For now, they are nonnegotiables. For example: *I know for sure that I am supposed to be at home with the kids right now rather than working full-time. I know for sure that graduate school is the right thing to pursue. I have no doubts that I need to be volunteering at the food pantry once a week.*

- **What are you currently doing that you could let go of if needed?** These are the events, projects, and commitments that are optional. If you find that you need to cut back on some things to accommodate any changes you want to make, these will be the first things to consider letting go of. For example: *I love my book club, but I could let it go if I need to create more space. I spend a lot of time volunteering at the kids' school. I love it, but I could cut back if I need to.*

- **What is the next big change or shift you anticipate? When do you think it will take place?** These are the changes you know are coming your way and that you definitely need to plan for. For example: *We'll have a new baby in six months. I start a new job after the first of the year. My mom is having surgery and will need extra care for a few weeks after she comes home from the hospital.*

STEP 3: Identify and Prioritize Your Pacesetters

Now that you have the big picture of the year ahead, it's time to consider how your pacesetters will impact your schedule. Where do they fit? What will it take to achieve wholeness in these key areas? This exercise will help you identify which pacesetters you need to prioritize and the action steps that will help you to move toward wholeness (*shalom*) in these areas of your life.

A. Identify Your Pacesetters

Take six to eight index cards and write down one pacesetter on the top of each card. For example, my cards this year included:

Work   *Body*
Relationships   *Spiritual vitality*

Other potential pacesetters could be anything that's important to you and reflective of this season in your life. For example:

New business endeavor   *Elderly parent needing extra care*
Child with special needs   *Additional education*
Home renovation project   *Career development opportunity*

The main idea is that pacesetters are things that set the pace of your life somehow. When you look at your schedule, you will need to allow time for these pacesetters and acknowledge any potential trade-offs you may need to make in order to accommodate them. If you need to eliminate some things you are currently involved in in order to make room for these pacesetters, that's okay. You can't squeeze your pacesetters into the margins of your life. Your priority pacesetters simply must get the first and best of your time and energy.

B. Imagine Wholeness

On each pacesetter card, write down how you define wholeness in that area. Then elaborate on your definition with some personal details. For example:

> *Work:* I am satisfied and content with one day's work, and I end each workday with some time and energy left over.
>
> *Relationships:* I am investing time with the right people, in the right place, at the right level.
>
> *Body:* I am proactive in prioritizing care of my body through nutrition, regular exercise, and preventative medical care.
>
> *Spiritual vitality:* My spiritual disciplines are life-giving and sustainable and create an environment in which ongoing spiritual growth is possible.
>
> *New business endeavor:* I am focusing on long-term measures of success and not discouraged by short-term setbacks.
>
> *Additional education:* I am investing the right energy and resources in the right educational track that will yield the greatest return.

Example:

Pacesetter: My inner circle relationships

Wholeness is: Investing time with the right people, in the right place, at the right level.

Personal details: My inner circle is my immediate family. I want to be fully present in my moments with them.

C. Set Goals and Identify Action Steps

On the back of each card, write down one potential goal for that pacesetter. (You'll identify goals for all of your pacesetters, but you'll eventually choose just one or two to focus on for the year.) Your goals represent a change you would like to make that will lead you toward wholeness in this area of your life. For example, a goal for inner circle relationships might be, "I will intentionally invest more time with my family by having dinner together once a week." For additional guidance in setting goals and in considering how goals might impact your relationships, see "SMART Goals" (page 210) and "The Relational Impact of Setting Goals" (page 211).

Now write down the action steps needed to accomplish your goal. What will it take to make your goal a reality? These are your action steps. For example:

- Get buy-in: I need to make sure everyone in my family is up for the challenge. Be flexible to change to every other week if needed to fit everyone's schedule.
- Identify the best night and time.
- Leave work early on family dinner night.

Example:

Main Goal

• *I will intentionally invest more time with my family by having dinner together once a week.*

Action Steps

• *Get buy-in: I need to make sure everyone in my family is up for the challenge. Be flexible to change to every other week if needed to fit everyone's schedule.*

• *Identify the best night and time.*

• *Leave work early on family dinner night.*

SMART GOALS

In setting goals, try to keep them **SMART**:

Specific: How will you define success for this goal? For example, "I want to be healthier" is a good objective but not a specific goal. Something like, "I want to lower my cholesterol," or "I want to work out regularly," are better goals because success is clearly defined.

Measurable: How will you know when you have achieved this goal? For example, "I want to lower my cholesterol by 30 points," or "I want to run three miles, four days a week."

Actionable: Is this goal something over which you have control? For example, a goal such as "I want my husband to be more spontaneous" is not actionable because it's not within your control—you can't *make* your husband do anything.

Realistic: Is this goal achievable? Good goals are both challenging *and* realistic. They inspire you, but also set you up for success! Unrealistic goals set you up for failure. For example, if your family rarely has dinner together, making your goal "dinner with the family every night" is probably not realistic. Starting with one night a week might be doable for now.

Time-Bound: What is the time frame for achieving your goal? For example, "within the next four weeks," "by May 15," or "by the end of the year." Without a target date, goals tend to become one more thing we need to do but never can seem to get around to. Set yourself up for success by setting a deadline.

THE RELATIONAL IMPACT
OF SETTING GOALS

Setting goals can be challenging because any time you make a change, the people closest to you are impacted by that change. Here are four questions to help you consider the potential impact your goals might have on your relationships.

- Who could be impacted if you take action on this goal?

- How might they be impacted (positively and negatively)?

- How do you expect them to respond? What if their response is not what you expect?

- How does what others think and feel affect how *you* feel about your goal?

D. Prioritize Your Pacesetters

Now that you've identified potential goals and action steps for each of your pacesetters, it's time to choose one or two pacesetters as your primary focus for the year ahead.

- Start by rereading each card. As you read, consider the impact this pacesetter might have on you. For example, how much value would it add to your life? How helpful would it be in moving you toward wholeness? How important is it to you?

- Set the cards on the table in front of you, placing each one in a column by order of importance. Put the most important cards on the top and those that are of lesser importance on the bottom. For example, if having a weekly sit-down dinner with your family would add the most value to your life right now, put that card at the top of the column. If balancing your work and family life could use some attention, but overall you feel okay about that aspect of your life, put that card at the bottom. For additional help with this part of the process, see "Assessing Your Pacesetters" (see below).

- Continue this process until you have worked through all the cards, making changes and adjustments in priority as you go.

Choose the two most important pacesetters and set them aside for now. You'll come back to them in step 5.[14]

ASSESSING YOUR PACESETTERS

If you are having trouble deciding which pacesetters to prioritize, here are some questions to help you think them through.

- Imagine you've just had an ideal week. Describe it. What are at least three things that happened that made it an ideal week?

- What are you tolerating or putting up with in your life right now? (Make a list.)

- What would you like more of in your life?

- What would you like less of in your life?

- What do you *want* in life but don't have?

- What do you *have* in life but don't want?

- What three things are you doing regularly that don't serve you well?

- What other areas of your life might be affected by this change?

- What is the price of making this change? Are you willing to pay the price?

- How might your life be better if you accomplish this goal?

- Are there any ways in which your life might be worse if you accomplish this goal?

- Are you able to complete this goal on your own, or do you need help from others? If necessary, what needs to change so that achieving this goal is within your control?

- If you experienced or achieved nothing else in the next year, what three things would still make the year a success for you?

STEP 4: Establish an Annual Rhythm

Think of this step as constructing the framework of the house you are building with your schedule. The framework marks out where the rooms will be and where the doors and windows will go; it gives you a basic idea of how everything will fit together in the end.

An annual rhythm reflects the different tempos of each season throughout the year, based on what's occurring in your personal and professional life. When you look at the scope of your year overall, you will find that a pattern of pacing naturally emerges.

- Open your calendar for the coming year and write in all the nonnegotiable events and commitments. This includes birthdays, holidays, and anniversaries. If you have school-age kids, mark in all the important school dates for your children, as well as any known extracurricular activities. Include dates and events connected to your inner-circle of friends as well any nonnegotiable work commitments.

- Briefly review each month and take note of any emerging patterns. In my case, the year's tempo alternates between fast-paced and slower-paced seasons that happen to coincide with the pace of the school year. As you look across the scope of your year, what rhythms do you see? What are your slow seasons and your fast seasons? In your journal or on a pad of paper, create a three-column chart to summarize the overall rhythm and tempo of your year. For example:

Time frame	Tempo	Description
August – October	Fast pace	Kids start school
November – January	Slow pace	Holiday season
February – May	Fast pace	Busy work season
June – July	Slow pace	Summer break

As much as I can, I try to honor the natural tempo of my year by building my schedule around the major milestones. There's already a natural pace and momentum to our schedules most of the time. If we try to work against it, we will only complicate our lives and put unnecessary roadblocks in our path. Instead, try to capitalize on the flow.

Part of the value of considering the overall rhythm of your year is to assess where you might have extra capacity to focus on pacesetters that require adding new activities to your schedule. For example, let's say you have the honor of hosting the family reunion this year. As you review your annual schedule, you notice that the summer months are slower. It makes sense to plan to host the reunion in the summer.

Another way you could find time and capacity for the family reunion is to make a trade-off. Let's say your great aunt, the visionary and driving force behind the event, declares that it must take place in the fall. If the fall is your busiest season, you might still be able to accommodate it if you make a trade-off. Are there events or commitments that could be postponed or removed in order to make space for the reunion? If so, that's a trade-off. Determining your trade-offs is an important part of planning for your annual rhythm.

When you identify a fast season, it's a good idea to identify why it's a fast season. For example, is it a busy season because of things you have no control over, such as your children's school activities or your personal work requirements? Or is it busy because you've scheduled too many activities and commitments? When we have a slow season, we could keep adding things and before we know it, it becomes fast! At some point, your schedule will get filled up. So as part of reviewing your annual rhythm, it's a good idea to identify the existing commitments over which you have the most control. What are your nonnegotiables? Prioritize what's most important to you so you know what you can and cannot trade off if you need to make a choice. Remember that you are aiming for wholeness, not only achievement or productivity. Establish what wholeness looks like for you and build your annual rhythm to accomplish this.

STEP 5: Set Your Pacesetters

Now that you have an idea of what your annual rhythm looks like, you can incorporate into your schedule your priority pacesetters (identified in step 3). While the annual rhythm provides the framework of our schedules, here we set the brick and mortar that complete the structure—the weekly and daily rhythms of our lives.

Your calendar is sacred space. Setting your pacesetters allows you to think through how they will best fit in this space. Here are four questions to consider as you set your pacesetters:

- *Is this pacesetter a daily, weekly, or annual rhythm?* For example, investing in inner-circle relationships might be a daily rhythm, while the soccer season or the women's retreat at church is an annual rhythm.

- *What personal strengths can I draw on to help me achieve my goals in this area?* Each of us possesses strengths that help us achieve what we want in life. These are the things that energize us, allow us to feel fulfilled, make a positive impact on others, and even make us feel strong. For example: *I am organized and adaptable. This will help me make room for more family time and help me to achieve my goal of making family dinner a weekly rhythm.*

- *What are some challenges I might face?* Working toward a goal will always require overcoming some difficulties. Go into this process anticipating potential hurdles so that you will be prepared for them. For example: *My work schedule is unpredictable at times. I need to remain organized. I need to remind myself to be satisfied with one day's work and have reserves left over at the end of each day.*

- *What compromises am I willing to make in order to move forward?* Compromise is not failure. Every compromise you make that moves you closer to your goal is progress. For example: *If my family members can't have dinner together once a week, we can start with every other week or monthly.*

Setting your pacesetters means there is an intentional place on your calendar for achieving the goal for this pacesetter. Let's revisit my example of having dinner with family once a week. It's one thing to set such a goal, but it's another thing entirely to make it happen consistently. For example, I know I will need to stop working earlier on those days, get buy-in from the family, and identify the best night for everyone. Other contingencies might have an impact on where dinner is placed in the schedule.

Even though the best night for family dinner for me might be Wednesday, that could also be the same night as the kids' youth group. Then, it's time to find a different night! Finally, we land on Thursday nights. Then this pacesetter is set on my weekly calendar.

Another example might be a goal to work out regularly. If this were your goal, you might consider why regular exercise has been difficult for you in the past. Was it the type of exercise, time of day, or maybe the gym location? Think about the factors that hinder or contribute to your ability to establish this as a regular rhythm. Then, place it on your schedule in a time and frequency that will set yourself up for success.

The placement of your pacesetter might sometimes depend on factors beyond your control. For example, let's say one of your pacesetters is caring for elderly parents and a goal is to accompany them to their doctor appointments. Setting this pacesetter in your schedule will depend on the doctor's availability and your parents' health needs. This pacesetter might be set on a monthly basis or intermittently throughout the year.

STEP 6: Establish Your Weekly Rhythm

To construct a weekly rhythm, take stock of what needs to happen regularly each week and prioritize those things on your calendar. As part of your weekly planning, make sure to allow adequate time for the following vital components:

- *A Sabbath zone:* A Sabbath zone is a defined period of rest and renewal. Ideally, this would be a twenty-four-hour period in which you refrain from work and chores and engage in activities you enjoy.

- *Priority pacesetters:* Add to your top two pacesetters from step 3 and the action steps associated with each goal into your schedule first.

- *Flex zone(s):* Flex zones are planned margin. Let's face it: most weeks don't go as planned. If every single minute of every day is maxed out, it's a setup for failure—and a lot of unnecessary stress. Flex zones provide some give-and-take time you can use for any unanticipated needs and to catch up on projects or to-do list tasks.

- *Weekend zone:* Weekend zones are times that are neither Sabbath nor work. They generally fall on the weekends (hence the term, "weekend zone"). For me, they are a catchall space I use to plan things like birthday celebrations, wedding or baby showers, events with the kids, working on home projects, personal care, and so on.

- *Look-ahead zone:* This is dedicated time to look ahead into the next week. Ideally, this should occur at the end of your work week. It could take one to two hours, depending on how complex the upcoming week is and how many adjustments need to be made. It's an opportunity to set your rhythms and make any necessary adjustments and trade-offs.

In your journal or on a pad of paper, create a seven-column chart to summarize your overall weekly rhythm. If either of your top two pacesetters is part of your weekly rhythm, include it as well as your Sabbath zone, flex zone, weekend zone, and look-ahead zone. Make sure that these components have a place in your weekly schedule before you add anything else. Below is an example of my weekly rhythm, which includes my new pacesetter goal of Thursday night family dinners.

Sunday	Monday	Tuesday	Wednesday	Thursday	Friday	Saturday
Church, work	Exercise, work	Exercise, late night at work	Connect Group, work	Exercise, work, family dinner	**Weekend Zone** This is a flex zone for work, family, errands, exercise, etc.	
				Look-Ahead Zone		
				Sabbath Zone Thursday 6:00 p.m. — Friday 2:00 p.m.		

STEP 7: Establish Your Daily Rhythms[15]

Having clarity about your priority pacesetters as well as your annual and weekly rhythms provides the essential big-picture framework to help you put your daily rhythms in context. It allows you to see the blueprint of what you are building before you choose the wall art. Your daily rhythms are the equivalent of the wall art, not the blueprint. That's why we work on the big-picture rhythms first. Remember too that if you have any monthly rhythms, be sure to account for them.

So now it's time to schedule your days. Begin with a generic template of your weekly structure. On a pad of paper or in your journal, create a two-column chart for each day of a typical week (example below). Block in your pacesetters first and then the big things you need to do every day. My daily tempo varies from a measured Sunday, to a fast-moving midweek, to a relatively slow weekend that can change at an instant if something unexpected comes up — which it often does. Here are a few daily rhythm examples from my week.

Sunday Rhythm

Time	Activity
7:00 a.m. – 9:00 a.m.	Wake up, prepare for the day
9:00 a.m. – 2:00 p.m.	Church
2:00 p.m. – 4:00 p.m.	Transition
4:00 p.m. – 7:00 p.m.	Catch up on work that needs to be completed before Monday.[16]
7:00 p.m. – 9:00 p.m.	Dinner, reset for the week. (Resetting for the week includes packing lunches, making sure school clothes are laundered, running errands for items needed for school and/or work, reviewing the calendar for the week and making any necessary adjustments.)

Monday Rhythm

Time	Activity
7:00 a.m. – 10:00 a.m.	Wake up, send kids off to school, devotions,[17] work out, get ready for work
10:00 a.m. – 5:00 p.m.	Work: Develop content for messages, book, staff development classes
5:00 p.m. – 9:00 p.m.	Transition, dinner and time with family

Thursday Rhythm

Time	Activity
7:00 a.m. – 10:00 a.m.	Wake up, send kids off to school, devotions, work out, get ready for work
10:00 a.m. – 4:00 p.m.	Work: Staff Meetings
4:00 p.m. – 6:00 p.m.	Transition, Look-ahead Zone
6:00 p.m.	Sabbath Zone begins

Planning ahead helps me identify what I need to trade off or if I have given myself enough flexibility just in case I am faced with an unexpected event. After completing the schedule for each day of the week, what do your daily and weekly schedules look like? You can use the sample template below and plan your own daily rhythm. Feel free to integrate in your own calendar afterwards.

Wrapping Up Your Reboot...

Now that you have your schedule set with regular rhythms and Sabbath zones, take a look at the big picture. Does it look like a manageable pace for you? At the end of this reboot process, you should have a good gauge of milestones that mark the rhythm of your year, as well as a manageable pace for your monthly commitments and the flow of each week.

Perhaps, if you're used to squeezing as much as you can into your schedule, there might be more white space than you are used to. This is okay. Trust the process you just worked through and settle into it for at least three to four months before making any significant changes. Take notes of what is and is not working along the way.

As you wrap up your reboot, consider practicing the habits of perspective discussed in chapter 10 (pages 156–58). Celebrate the good things and release the past. Renew your vision for the future. Realign your present circumstances with the future you envision. Be sure to refocus on *shalom*, the big picture of what wholeness means for you. Write your reflections in your journal and refer to them when you do your next reboot.

The reboot process is not meant to confine or imprison you in a strict grid. It's a process that serves to equip you to honor the sanctity of time. As you finish building your schedule, release it to God and trust Him to give you the grace to live it out. Through God's guidance and direction, you can become proactive in building the life you want with *shalom* as the end result.

Additional Bible Translation Copyright Notices

Notes

1. See the title of the book by Cornelius Plantinga, *Not the Way It's Supposed to Be: A Breviary of Sin* (Grand Rapids: Eerdmans, 1996).
2. Ann Spangler and Lois Tverberg, *Sitting at the Feet of Rabbi Jesus: How the Jewishness of Jesus Can Transform Your Life* (Grand Rapids: Zondervan, 2009), 135–37.
3. See http://www.jewfaq.org/shabbat.htm (accessed March 24, 2014).
4. Adapted from http://www.thefreedictionary.com/tension (accessed March 25, 2014).
5. This section is adapted from a sample report created in October 2011 by Ellen Eernst Kossek for The Center for Creative Leadership, available at www.ccl.org/leadership/pdf/assessments/WLIFeedback.pdf (accessed March 25, 2014).
6. See www.rzim.org/a-slice-of-infinity/god-and-body/ (accessed March 25, 2014), italics in original.
7. Abraham Joshua Heschel, *The Sabbath* (New York: Farrar, Straus and Giroux, 1951, 1979, 2005), 6.
8. Ibid., 8.
9. Ibid.
10. The reboot instructions assume that you are engaging this process at or near the beginning of a new year. However, it works just as well no matter when you decide to do it. Wherever you are in the year, just look ahead at the next twelve months. For example, if you happen to be rebooting in May, use the beginning of May this year to the end of April next year as your time frame. It will work just fine.

11. A great resource for further study and guidance on finding your purpose is Rick Warren's book, *The Purpose-Driven Life* (Grand Rapids: Zondervan, 2002). I encourage you to check out this book if you haven't already. This will be a journey in itself to prepare you for future opportunities.

12. For an overview of the reboot process, see chapter 10, pages 147–52.

13. The instructions for the reboot assume that you are engaging this process at or near the beginning of a new year. However, it works just as well no matter when you decide to do it. Wherever you are in the year, just look ahead at the next twelve months. For example, if you happen to be rebooting in May, use May this year to April next year as your time frame. It will work just fine.

14. Your top priority pacesetters should reflect and support your theme for the year. If you had difficulty identifying your theme in step 1, or if your theme now feels somewhat disconnected from your priority pacesetters, this is a good time to go back and update your theme.

15. For additional guidance on scheduling, see "Eight Key Tips for Scheduling" in chapter 10, pages 153–155.

16. Sunday counts as a workday for me, which is why there is space on this day for work-related tasks.

17. Spiritual vitality is a key part of my daily rhythm. It's time set aside each day to be with God. If your schedule permits, start your day with Bible engagement, prayer, and journaling. If first thing in the morning doesn't work for you, find another time slot that is a better fit for you.